7 Dirty Secrets of a Strong Black Woman

Dr. Rhonda Thompson Alexander

PUBLISHING CO.
a IUVO Consulting Company
Virginia Beach, VA, USA
www.soulscribe.net

Other works by Dr. Alexander

EntrHERpreneur: The Woman's Journey to Discovering & Embracing the Call to Entrepreneurship

Your Life's Calling: Maximizing What's Within to Engage Your Calling and Reach Your Destiny

Side-Hustle or Sustainable: A Book to Help You Determine Whether Your New Business Is a Hobby or A Sustainable Business Venture

7 Dirty Secrets of a Strong Black Woman
By Dr. Rhonda Thompson Alexander

SoulScribe Publishing Co.
P.O. Box 56436
Virginia Beach, VA 23456
USA
www.soulscribe.net

© 2025 by Rhonda Alexander
All rights reserved.
No part of this book may be reproduced or transmitted by any person or entity, including internet search engines and retailers, in any form or by any means, electronic or mechanical, including photocopying, recording, scanning or by any information storage and retrieval system without the prior written permission of the author of this book.
Where quotations have been used, the author has used all reasonable endeavors to ensure that the materials are not in breach of copyright and intellectual property laws.

Cover images by Mykahl Raphael Creative Agency (www.mykahlraphael.com)
Visit the author's website: www.TheDrRhonda.com

USA ISBN: 979-8-9924924-0-8
Printed in the United States of America

This book is dedicated to every Black woman who has contributed in any way to my becoming the woman I am today. This book is also in honor of my grandmothers and my great-grandmothers – truly phenomenal Black women, whose legacies I have the honor of carrying. A special dedication goes to my mom. Thanks, Mommie, for walking this journey with me.

Contents

Part 1: The Secrets

Part 2: How Did We Get Here?

Part 3: The Truth

Foreword

Ladies, imagine this: we're gathered in a luxurious, five-star resort perched on plush white couches. Glasses of wine and hot tea in hand, laughter and knowing nods flowing freely as we trade stories of triumph and pain, ambition and exhaustion, courage and vulnerability. The ocean whispers in the background, but it's no match for the rhythm of our voices—strong, unapologetic, beautifully intertwined.

This setting might seem idyllic, but I'm struck by how seamlessly it mirrors the journey of reading *7 Dirty Secrets of a Strong Black Woman* by Dr. Rhonda Thompson Alexander. When I read the prelude chapter, I was floored. Through tear-blurred eyes, I whispered, "I didn't give Rhonda permission to write a book about me." That's how personal, raw, and unnervingly accurate this work is.

Rhonda doesn't just write; she unveils. She exposes the truths we carry like well-worn handbags—the silent battles and quiet triumphs of women who are both the backbone and the beating heart of their families and communities. She writes the story of the woman who juggles every responsibility yet secretly wonders if she'll ever be enough, the woman who smiles through heartbreak and her secret tears, the woman who achieves, leads, nurtures, and inspires while feeling utterly invisible in her most vulnerable moments. And if you're like me, her words will grip you by the shoulders and demand that you sit with truths you've kept buried too long.

One of the most profound gifts of this book is its audacity to dismantle the myth of the invincible Black woman. For centuries, we've been told—implicitly and explicitly—that our strength is our most valuable currency. We've worn the cape, carried the weight, and pressed forward because our mothers, grandmothers, and ancestors modeled nothing less. And while there is honor in resilience, Rhonda dares to ask, "At what cost?"

Each chapter feels like a mirror, reflecting the complexities of our identities. Whether she speaks of heartbreak that left her unmoored, the pressure to excel in spaces that don't affirm us, or the searing loneliness masked by busy schedules, her words feel like a sacred invitation to unmask and breathe. They say, "Sis, you're not alone. And it's okay to take the cape off."

But this book isn't just about excavating pain; it's about liberation. Rhonda takes us on a journey to reclaim ourselves. She reminds us that strength doesn't mean self-neglect, and independence doesn't mean isolation. She shows us that vulnerability is not a liability but a superpower. Through her words, we're encouraged to redefine what strength means for us in this season of life.

As I read, I could feel the sisterhood this book creates. I envisioned us—Black women across the spectrum of experience—holding space for each other. We are laughing, crying, and exhaling as Rhonda gives us the language to articulate feelings we've suppressed for years. She reminds us of the beauty of softness, the necessity of community, and the healing that comes when we finally lay down the burdens we were never meant to carry alone.

As a woman of faith, this message spoke directly to my relationship with God through Jesus Christ. Scripture teaches us to cast our burdens on Him because He cares for us (1 Peter 5:7). Rhonda's words are a gentle yet powerful reminder of the strength we find when we lean into grace and trust God's care for every part of our lives, and they beautifully invite readers to explore that truth for themselves.

This book isn't just a good read; it's a clarion call to step boldly into the journey of wholeness, anchored in the assurance that God's strength is made perfect in our weakness (2 Corinthians 12:9). Rhonda challenges us to acknowledge the weight we carry and invites us to pursue a life where thriving replaces mere survival.

I wish I had *7 Dirty Secrets of a Strong Black Woman* years ago. It's the kind of book that feels like a long-overdue conversation with your best girlfriends. It's the wisdom of a big sister who has walked through the fire and emerged stronger, softer, and freer. It's the encouragement we didn't know we needed, delivered with the compassion and boldness only Rhonda can bring.

So, pour yourself a glass of wine or freshly steeped tea into your favorite mug (whichever suits your vibe), find a cozy spot, and prepare to be seen, heard, challenged, and empowered. Rhonda has written a love letter to us—Black women who feel we carry the world on our shoulders.

As you turn each page, remember this:

You are not alone.

You are enough.

And it's time to redefine what strength really means.

With love and solidarity,

Dr. Synetheia N. Newby

Preface

You're about to embark on a journey. This isn't just "some book" I wrote, this is part memoir and part motivation – but all movement. When I set out on this project, I didn't realize how much it would change me in the process. Quite honestly, I thought I was going to share a few secrets, give a few tips, and help some people along the way. Boy was I wrong!

The more I wrote, the deeper I was required to go. In fact, some of the secrets I share in the pages to come, I'd never talked about publicly. But going through those old memories and digging around in those old feelings helped me to experience healing on a whole new level. You won't find me simply giving you advice for ditching strong Black womanhood, you're going to discover all the ways I was the poster child for it myself.

I've described this book on several occasions as "real" and "raw", and I want you to know those aren't just attention-grabbing adjectives. I've taken my hair out of the bun, I've set down the fancy glasses, and I've come from behind the titles and degrees. So, while you may get a bit of "The Doctor" toward the end of the book, more than anything, you're just going to get me – Rhonda.

Preface

In my other books, I come to you in the role and the tone of "coach" – the one who has the expertise to show you how to transform your business, your book, or your life. But with this book, I needed to do something different, so I decided to just be myself. I wanted to share my stories with you in a tone that felt more like sister-friends sitting on the couch – comfy and cozy – with our favorite beverage in hand.

So, you'll find there are no pretenses here. I committed to being open and honest with this book in ways I never have before, and to do that, I had to create a space that was safe enough for us to have the conversation. Even though I may not get to hear your stories, I wanted you to know that the space you're entering is safe enough for you to reflect on and release your own secrets, too.

Trigger Warnings & Disclaimers

The stories you'll read are about my experiences and my feelings as I went through them. This book isn't a tell-all or an exposé, so if you're looking for a book that spills tea or puts other folks' business out there, you'll be sorely disappointed. Instead, what you'll find is my vulnerability and my honesty about some of the major moments of my life from my point of view.

I'll give you the trigger warnings now – there are themes of grief and abuse – both physical and sexual – in this book. Of course, there's nothing graphic, but you should know, so you're not blindsided, in case that's a sensitive area for you. At the same time, there are themes of profound discovery and healing too. And if I'm honest, a few times, the "corny" side of me found its way out – I couldn't resist. (I'm being me, remember?!)

Just know that this isn't a trauma dump. My prayer is that you'll laugh and discover insights about your own strength as you read. And if, at some point, you also find tears streaming down your face, it's ok. The same thing happened to me while writing. I'll pass you the tissues.

Now when it comes to the way the book has been written – it might be a little different than what you'd expect. The first seven chapters consist of my 7 Dirty Secrets. This is where I take you on a tour of my life and share with you how I ended up with a version of strength so toxic it almost killed me. The last 7 chapters are the opposites of those secrets – the truths – they're where I get to tell you how I overcame the pain I've experienced, how I released my secrets, and how you can do the same.

I encourage you to read the book in the order of each of the chapters – I promise you, it's a journey, and I do not leave you hanging. I want you to find the same healing I've found, even though your secrets are undoubtedly different from mine.

The last thing you should know is that I've prayed over this book. I've prayed that we'll all find the healing and freedom we were destined to experience before the world began. I've prayed that as I share my heartbreaks and triumphs, you'll find the courage to discover and share yours, too. And finally, I've prayed that you'll find your voice again – that you'll find you again. That this book will be the key that releases you from the silence you've kept for so long, and that you'll discover all the new ways to soar – to love yourself better and more deeply than you ever have.

I believe with all my heart that freedom waits for you in these pages, and as you turn this one and embark on this journey with me, may your life reach new heights and never be the same again.

All my best,
Rhonda

PRELUDE

The Breaking Point

"I think I'm broken."

In the aftermath, those were the only words I could muster to explain how I felt.

Just days before, I'd collected myself from the floor of the bathroom after what could only be called a "big breakdown" – the mother of all panic attacks. It was unlike anything I'd ever experienced before. I'd heard about people having "nervous breakdowns", but I never imagined myself in that place.

For almost a year leading up to that night, I'd been trapped in an unrelenting state of overwhelm and functional depression. I was grappling with the devastating loss of two very close relationships, watching my businesses unravel right before my eyes, and stretching myself way too thin, trying to keep everything from falling apart. I was running on empty and trying to pour from a cup that was bone dry. The losses had been

Prelude: The Breaking Point

unexpected and heartbreaking, and they'd left me feeling isolated and grief-stricken. These weren't just relationships; they were core pieces of my life that had kept me grounded. Suddenly, my support system, my sense of community, and my emotional anchors were gone, and I found myself "out there" – trying to stay afloat. Friends we once shared grew distant, and I felt out of place nearly everywhere I went. All at once, it seemed I didn't belong anywhere anymore. The loneliness was suffocating, and it drained my energy in ways I couldn't have imagined.

My personal life was a mess, but my business life was no better. Despite all the planning and hard work I'd put into my businesses, both ventures were flat-lining. No matter what strategy I tried or how much coaching I got, nothing seemed to work. Revenue plummeted, and the more I tried to fix things, the worse they became. I felt like I was doing jumping jacks in quicksand, with every leap sinking me deeper into failure. Every day, I'd wake up with a deep sense of dread, wondering if this would be the day I'd have to accept defeat.

To make matters worse, things were going very wrong at one of the organizations I was leading. It was going through a transition, and the environment had become unexpectedly toxic and hostile. I was caught in the middle of a battlefield where my presence and expertise were being questioned and undermined. I found myself embattled, second-guessing every decision, and doubting my own abilities. It just felt like everywhere I looked, there was chaos, and it seemed as if I couldn't do anything right.

I was working 80 to 90 hours a week by then – sometimes more – pushing myself to the absolute limit and getting nowhere. Exhaustion had become my new normal. I'd show up to meetings with a smile on my face, only to collapse into bed each night, feeling worse than I had when I'd awakened.

And then my health took a turn for the worse. I was constantly weak and fatigued, unable to muster the strength for even basic tasks. I'd get dizzy just trying to hold a conversation. My heart felt like it was running a marathon: skipping beats, racing, and pounding hard. Each night, I'd go to bed wondering if my heart would give out while I slept. In the morning,

I'd wake up surprised – sometimes annoyed – that I was still alive to face another awful day.

This went on for weeks.

By the time I saw my cardiologist, I was desperate for answers. After a heart monitor and a series of tests, she told me my heart was fine. I couldn't believe it. Fine? No, that couldn't be right. I felt like I was dying every day! I needed a diagnosis, a clear explanation for what was happening to me. But I got nothing. It felt like I was being told I was imagining things, like maybe I was exaggerating. I was furious, frustrated, and felt more alone than ever.

The night of the breakdown, I had hit my limit. I was lying on the couch, and the palpitations had gotten out of control. My heart was hammering like it was trying to beat its way out of my chest. My entire body was trembling, and my thoughts were racing.

What first came to mind was my daughter and all the moments I would miss. And what would she do without me? Then, I thought about my dear family, my friends, and the life I still desired to live. I wasn't ready to go! But it seemed like this was it. I'd pushed myself too far, and now I was at the end.

And that's when the anger hit. It bubbled up from somewhere deep, and it felt like an explosion in my chest. I was mad at God, mad at myself, mad at everyone who'd ever let me feel like I had to handle everything on my own. This wasn't fair. None of it was fair. I was tired of being strong, tired of pretending, tired of feeling like I had to hold it all together while I was falling apart inside.

I snapped.

I screamed into the empty room. I threw things. I cussed and swore at God, at life, at the people who had let me down and made me feel small and insignificant. I had a full-blown tantrum, and there was no one there to stop me. I'd been there for everyone – solving their problems,

Prelude: The Breaking Point

encouraging them, holding them up. But now, when I needed someone, there was nobody. No one. I felt abandoned and betrayed.

"I can't do this anymore!" I screamed. "This isn't fair, and I'm done with all of it!"

I could barely breathe. My skin felt too tight, like I needed to peel myself out of my own body. I made it to the bathroom, sobbing uncontrollably. I couldn't stop. I'd completely lost control and had no idea how to get it back. The sobs turned into hyperventilation. I couldn't seem to get enough air. I laid down on the cold, hard floor, convinced I was going to die right there, with no one to find me.

And then I thought: *"Maybe I <u>want</u> to die."*

The idea of suicide scared me, and it made me cry out for help. To God. To my neighbors. To somebody. Anybody. But no one came.

By the time the rage finally burned out, I was a whimpering, shaking mess. I crawled from the bathroom to the bed and wept until I simply couldn't anymore. Before I finally fell asleep from exhaustion, I managed to send one text:

"I can't live like this."

***

The next morning, I woke up feeling completely drained. Every muscle ached, and my head was pounding. I was empty, like a balloon that had been deflated. I didn't feel relief, though. Just numb. If anything, a deep sadness had settled into my bones – a kind of despair that left me wondering if I'd ever feel like myself again. My body felt foreign, as if it had betrayed me in some way.

And in a sense, it had. But I hadn't left it much of a choice. I'd been pushing myself so hard, ignoring every warning sign, and now my body was demanding that I listen. The problem was, I didn't know how to listen. I had been so focused on *doing* – on meeting every demand, juggling every responsibility, and showing up for everyone – that I'd forgotten how to just *be*.

At our next session, I told my therapist about the breakdown. I wasn't sure how to explain it, so I just said, "I think I'm broken." That's how it felt – like something had shattered inside me, and I couldn't put the pieces back together. For days, I tried to resume work as normal and just couldn't. I'd stare at the computer for hours, unable to do much more than scroll social media or the news. I couldn't seem to muster the brain power to do actual work.

My therapist looked at me with deep concern and suggested that I allow her to reach out to my mother. I didn't want her to. I didn't want anyone to know what had happened to me. But she insisted, and I agreed. Listening to them talk, I felt like a child again, caught and in trouble at school. There I was, a grown woman, sitting in therapy, and yet I felt like I was being scolded for something I couldn't control. But it wasn't a scolding I heard – it was fear. I hadn't just scared myself with what I'd experienced; I had frightened my therapist, too.

Soon, both of my parents were at my house. We sat down, and it was time for me to come clean. Through tears, I poured out everything – the breakdown, the overwhelm, the pain of losing people I loved, the failures in my businesses, the constant weight I'd been carrying.

It was like opening a floodgate. All the emotions I'd been trying to bottle up came rushing out. And my parents – thank God for them – sat there and listened. They didn't judge or try to fix it right away. They just listened. I hadn't realized how much I'd been hiding, even from them. Here they were, living just a few minutes down the road, and they had no idea what I was going through. I'd been carrying all of it alone and showing up like nothing was wrong.

My therapist and my parents worked together, helping me determine the next steps I'd take toward recovery. I knew I couldn't do this on my own, and they made it clear I didn't have to. They rallied around me, offering support, but more importantly, helping me craft a plan to get out of this mess. They encouraged me to reach out to my doctor and to other loved ones, so that I could lean on people who actually cared about me, even though I'd convinced myself no one did. Slowly, I began to accept help.

It was a wake-up call. I discovered that I didn't have to be the strong one all the time. I realized that I didn't have to carry the weight of the world on my shoulders – that I could fall apart and ask for help, and doing so didn't make me weak. It just made me human.

After that day, I took nearly six weeks off from everything. I didn't work. I didn't take on any new problems or projects. I sat and looked out the window. I found a tv series to binge watch. I avoided social media. I slept. My strength was gone, and I wasn't even sure I wanted it back.

How Did I Get Here?

I asked myself that question a lot during my time off. I had taken on too much and given too much of myself without replenishing. I hadn't properly grieved the losses I'd experienced, and I was taking care of everything and everyone except me. I was carrying the weight of my entire world, and it had crushed me.

And then it hit me: I had been hiding. Not just from others, but from myself. From my pain. From my fears. From everything I didn't want to confront. I'd been keeping myself busy, pouring everything I had into everyone else, because it was easier than sitting with my own emotions and acknowledging just how hurt I felt inside.

That's why the breakdown was more than just a moment of emotional exhaustion. It was the culmination of decades of self-sacrifice, of pushing past my own needs, and pretending I was fine. I'd been terrified that if I admitted how overwhelmed I was or how alone I felt, I'd be seen as weak, as not good enough. I thought I had to be invincible – unbreakable – because that's what everyone expected from me.

From the outside, I was the epitome of success and confidence, the one people looked to for guidance and strength. But inside, I was the complete opposite. It wasn't just the loss of relationships, the failing businesses, or the burnout. It was the accumulation of years of silencing my own voice, of holding back my own truth, and of hiding my pain behind a mask of perfection.

The trauma I'd experienced as a child, which I'd carefully buried and pretended didn't exist, was alive and well in my everyday life, unbeknownst to me. I thought I'd dismissed it and moved past it. But I hadn't. The shame and secrecy around those early experiences had created a pattern in my life – one that I couldn't see until now. Every time I didn't speak up for myself, every time I didn't hold space for my own needs, I was reinjuring that old childhood wound. I was reinforcing the muzzle that was keeping me silent, when I should have been shouting from the rooftops, "I matter, too!"

Silence is the Killer

Here's the thing: when you spend your life suppressing your voice, it doesn't just disappear. It turns inward. It becomes self-doubt, self-criticism, and overthinking. It wasn't unusual for that voice to haunt me late into the night, replaying the conversations of the day, picking apart everything I'd said and done, worrying that I'd made a mistake or let someone down. Every new project, every new role felt like a test I was doomed to fail. If someone questioned my decisions or pushed back on my ideas, I'd be triggered, sent into a spiral of self-doubt that could last for days.

It's exhausting living like that – always on edge, always second-guessing yourself, always feeling like an imposter in your own life. It took hitting rock bottom to realize that I had become a master of self-sacrifice – always putting others' needs before my own, always pushing through pain and exhaustion, always looking for validation and approval. I discovered that when you constantly put others before yourself, when you prioritize everyone else's comfort, happiness, and approval over your own, you give away parts of yourself that you can't get back. You silence your own voice to make space for theirs. You deny your own needs, your own desires, your own truth, until there's nothing left of you.

Prelude: The Breaking Point

I realized that my breakdown wasn't as much about everything I was dealing with in the present as it was about all the things I hadn't dealt with in the past. It was a lifetime of holding my breath, of biting my tongue, and of trying to be what I thought I was expected to be.

That's what trauma does. It lies to you and steals your voice. It makes you believe that speaking up is dangerous, that showing your true self is a risk you can't afford to take. It convinces you that silence is the only thing that can keep you safe. But you're not safe. You're imprisoned – locked into toxic cycles of self-sabotage, unable to break free.

The more I thought about it, the clearer it became. That pattern – the constant self-sacrifice, the people-pleasing, the overachieving – was rooted in a fear of rejection. I was afraid that if I didn't do enough, be enough, *give* enough, I'd be abandoned. I'd be alone. So, I kept giving until there was nothing left to give. And still, it didn't feel like enough. It *never* felt like enough.

I'm Not Alone in This.

So many women – especially Black women – carry the weight of these expectations. We feel like we have to be everything to everyone, all the time – no days off. We have to be strong, resilient, unbreakable, even when we're in shambles inside.

Indeed, we've become experts at projecting an image of "having it all together". We're the most educated demographic, with many of us being the highest earner in our homes; we're building powerhouse businesses, and we're transforming our communities. We're flaunting our Black Girl Magic and reveling in our ageless beauty, yet behind the scenes, many of us feel nothing like the person the world perceives us to be.

That's because as beautiful, intelligent, and accomplished as we are, many of us are secretly hiding pain and unresolved trauma that we need to address and heal.

Don't get me wrong - I'm not saying we're at fault. In truth, we were taught to hide it all. Our foremothers told us that time would heal all our wounds.

All we had to do was be strong, stuff down our secret pains – or ignore them altogether – and they would eventually go away.

But they didn't.

Instead, they became ever increasing weights we've dragged through our lives, and now we're exhausted. We've looked to self-care and self-help for relief, but the heaviness always seems to return. People look at us and praise us for being Strong Black Women, but what we hear is: *"You make carrying a lifetime of crap look good."*

Ask any of us and we'll tell you that today's definition of "strength" is not the flex it once was. It doesn't feel like courage, resilience, and tenacity anymore. These days, it's marked by pain, trauma, secrecy and the requirement to be perfect.

Vulnerability feels like a luxury we can't afford, and showing any kind of weakness seems like a betrayal to our legacy. So, we push ourselves, even when it's killing us.

We hide behind our accomplishments, thinking that if we just achieve more, if we just work harder, we'll finally prove our worth. But it's never enough. The world keeps asking for more. So, we keep giving.

And then we break.

When we finally reach our limit, it's devastating because we've spent our whole lives building up this façade of strength, of perfection. But here's the good news: We don't have to be perfect to be worthy. We don't have to sacrifice ourselves to be loved. We don't have to carry the weight of the world to prove that we're strong.

Strength can't be defined anymore by how much we can carry; it should reflect how much we refuse to. Real strength should be a demonstration of self-awareness – knowing what we have the capacity to carry, and what we do not. It's the recognition that your needs are just as important as everyone else's, and that taking care of yourself is not selfish – *it's necessary*.

Prelude: The Breaking Point

I had to learn that the hard way. I had to reach my breaking point to realize that I was carrying way too much, holding onto things I should have released a long time ago. Much of it was stuff I was never meant to carry in the first place. I had to lose my voice to understand just how much I needed it. I discovered that when you lose your voice – when you silence your truth – you're not the only one who's affected. The people around you are affected, too. The way you see and interact with the world becomes tainted – including the way you show up in your relationships and the way you live your life.

That's why it's so important for us to step out of the silence of secret-keeping and raise our voices. It's the only way we can step into our truth – by owning our stories and refusing to be defined by our trauma. It's *choosing* to be seen, even when it's uncomfortable, and allowing yourself to be vulnerable, even when it's scary.

The world doesn't need more perfect people. It needs more *real* people. Those who are willing to show up as they are, flaws and all, and say, "I'm not hiding anymore."

So, that's what I'm doing. I'm choosing to show up, to speak up, and to let go of the silence that has kept me playing small for so long. I'm choosing to be real, to be messy, and to be honest about what I've been through. Because that's the only way to heal. That's the only way to move forward.

It's not easy. There are days I still struggle, when I want to put the mask back on, hide in the background, and pretend that everything is fine. But I remind myself that strength doesn't pretend. It confronts pain, faces fears, and does the hard work of healing.

And that's what I'm inviting you to do, too. This book isn't just a memoir. It's an invitation to take an honest look at the places where you've been hiding, too – the areas where you've been sacrificing yourself for the sake of others. It will encourage you to examine yourself and ask, "Is this really who I want to be?"

If you find that the answer is no, then this book will also help you make a change. It will challenge you to let go of the toxic definition of strength that has kept you bound and silent, so you can embrace a new kind of strength – one that comes from within and liberates. A strength that honors your voice, your needs, and your worth.

Because you *are* worthy, you know. Just as you are.

It's about time we step out of the shadows and into the light. The world needs to see a new version of us – the one where they encounter our *real* selves.

You know – the one with no secrets.

Part 1

The Secrets

SECRET 1

I Refuse to Be a Victim

Rhonda.

That's what I was called when I came into the world.

It made sense. Firstborn to Ronald and Frances, I am the namesake – the junior, if you will. As the country was celebrating its bicentennial anniversary, this little girl entered the world with so much potential – a blank slate of possibility and opportunity. For three years, I was an only child, adored by my mother, cherished by my father. I wouldn't get my first sibling – Micahl – until 1979 and my second, Ben, until 1986.

To say that I was born into a large family would be an understatement. I had two sets of living great-grandparents, both sets of grandparents, and more aunts, uncles, and cousins than I can name or count. My great-grandmother, Rosa Wilkins (aka Mom-mo) was a pioneer of her time and the most likely source of my entrepreneurial spirit. She was a female pastor who built and grew a ministry in the 1950s, at a time when women did very little without the approval or permission of a man. But she did it. She commissioned the building of a church that still stands today, even though she is long gone.

On my mother's side, I was a first – the first great-grand to Rosa and Ben, first grand to Mable and Frank, and first child to Ronald and Frances. There are probably folks who would assume that I was spoiled as a result, and while I won't ever admit to that, I will say that I was well attended to. From my great-grands down, I was loved. I know that not every kid has the opportunity to braid her great-grandmother's hair or have her great-grandad read Dr. Seuss' *There's a Wocket in My Pocket* – or the way he read it, *There's a Wooket In My Pooket*, which to this day makes me snicker – but I did, and as an adult, I cherish those childhood moments.

My grandparents meant a lot to me. I don't know how my mother and father made it happen, but we had close bonds with both sides of our family. Those Christmases anticipating the arrival of Santa at Grammie and Grandaddy's house were the absolute highlight of the year because even though he came to our home on Christmas eve, we also knew that he went there and left us gifts too. As adults, though we clearly understand who and what Santa is, we still get excited when we see gifts from him under the tree. And our kids do, too. It's just one of the traditions that has survived the passing of time and of my loved ones.

Leaving Grammie and Granddaddy's house we'd end up at Grandma and Grandad's house – my dad's parents, Louise and Arthur – and that's where the fun and laughter were. My father was born second-to-last of six kids, and each of them would come to Virginia Beach with their families for the holidays. And while there weren't many physical presents passed around, there was always food and a whole heap of loud raucous laughter. My father's side of the family – also quite large – is where I learned to hold my own with cousins whose jokes could draw tears if you didn't have a good comeback. And when we weren't joking on each other, we were finding ways to have a good time.

The family gatherings on the Thompson side are also marked by the most amazing southern food. My Grandma, a South Carolinian, always cooked the most delicious dishes, but she is best known for her pots of chicken and rice. Of course, I'll never be able to cook on the same level as her, but I can say that I am the reigning chicken and rice champion – beating out my dad and other family members who dared to recreate her coveted secret recipe.

We always knew how dinners at the Thompson household would go. Grandad would sit at the head and my grandmother, parents, aunts, and uncles would sit at the table. The kids ate in the den – or wherever we could find a spot. Before dinner began, though, we'd all stand around the table and Grandad would pray over the food. Those prayers were never short. We kids would have one eye open, trying to sneak food or stifle giggles because Grandad had gotten emotional.

That's the thing about church kids – we're absolutely brutal. We had seen Grandad get emotional talking about his love for God and during prayer moments at church -- as a deacon, he was often called to pray the morning prayer. And by the time we were clowning teenagers, we knew exactly what was coming after his trademark "Dear Lord…" – tears.

Back then it was funny because we found ways to make fun of everything and everyone in church. I mean, when you spend 90% of your time there, what else would there be to do? Anyone who grew up in church knows the kids learn all the shouts, they know who's going to fall out or knock something over, and they can usually preach the Sunday sermons as well as the pastor. It comes with the territory.

Beyond regular church attendance, my family carries a rich legacy of faith. Both of my grandfathers served as respected deacons, and the matriarchs have long been known as devoted women of faith. In fact, nearly everyone in my family preaches, sings, or plays an instrument. So, we didn't just attend church; we were the church.

This legacy passed down to us is one of deep love and reverence for God, along with a strong commitment to serve in His church. And it began at birth. My parents dedicated me back to God – a tradition some faiths call christening, but in ours, it's known simply as dedicating. I know they couldn't fathom what lay ahead for my life, but this simple act marked their belief that no matter what happened to me, God would be fully in control, and He would protect and provide for me. Those early prayers made a difference, I believe, knowing what I know now, 48 years later. Those prayers invoked a hedge of protection that I'd need sooner than they could have imagined.

On The Other Hand

The Thompson homestead was filled with laughter and love, but it held some shadows, too. Despite the home's joy and warmth, trauma managed to find its way inside. Over the years, my grandparents fostered many children, one of whom was Jeffery, a young man around 16 years old. I was about three when he came to live with them. I don't know what brought him to their home, but I can only imagine he had his own painful story.

On the days both of my parents worked, I would stay with Grandma. She'd spend time each day working in the garden, and I'd remain inside watching TV. This would leave Jeffery and me – 3-year-old Rhonda – in the house…alone. He'd wait until my grandmother was busy outside to approach me to perform sexual acts on him. Of course, being three, I had no idea whether this was right or wrong, but I didn't like it, and I didn't want to do it. He never forced himself on me, but he'd tease me – calling me a baby – if I declined or complained. And of course, being a "big girl" at that age, I didn't want to be called a baby, so I'd relent and do as he'd asked.

I don't remember how long this went on, but I know it happened more than once. It became a game of dread for me – knowing the moment we were alone, he'd be back. There was no penetration, but other things happened, and it made me feel gross and scared.

I didn't know enough to tell my parents on my own, though I can remember being caught in my brother's crib doing something inappropriate. My father sat me down at the kitchen table and asked me where I'd gotten that from, and I told him that it was what the boy had done to me. I don't recall my father's response or his reaction, but I do know that the boy went away, and I didn't see him again until years later when I was perhaps 7 or 8 years old.

The moment I saw him, I hid. I hadn't seen him in several years, but I knew it was him – he had a certain way of biting his bottom lip, and that's what gave him away. I knew that he'd done something bad to me and I was afraid to be near him. I didn't want him to talk to me because I remembered what he usually asked for, so I stayed away, and I made sure that we didn't have any direct interaction. But that moment was memorable enough that today, I could tell you what he was wearing that day and where I hid.

I'm Not That Girl

Sometime during my teen years, I learned he died.

Oddly enough, I didn't feel anything about his death – no sadness, no anger. And, honestly, I'd never thought about what he'd done to me with any emotion attached to it. As I aged, any time I'd recall the abuse, I'd tell myself it didn't matter, because I wasn't a victim. I refused to let him contaminate me with that word. If there was anything dirty about what had happened, it was the fact that his actions put an unwanted – and disgusting – label on me: victim.

In my mind, victims were weak and powerless. I was neither of those things and promised myself I'd never be. So, I pretended the abuse never happened. I tucked those memories away and pushed on with life, believing that I'd somehow beaten the odds because I wasn't "damaged" by what happened.

But I was damaged. And the pain took root deep inside me, shaping how I saw myself and others. I avoided talking about the abuse because doing so would mean accepting a label I didn't want. And I couldn't bear that.

Because I refused to acknowledge what happened to me, I wasn't prepared for how it would impact every relationship I'd have in my life. I couldn't see how my inability to say "no" throughout my adult life would stem from the time I couldn't say "no" as a little girl. I couldn't foresee that my tendencies to stay in toxic situations and endure mistreatment were tied to my childhood instinct to freeze up and comply rather than speak out and protect myself. And because I couldn't see those things from the appropriate perspective, I thought I was weak. I didn't know I was dealing with the residue of what had been done to me.

This Is How It Starts

My silence wasn't strength. It was submission. The more I submitted to silence, the more I gave my power away. My trauma, like the trauma of so many other women, was the beginning of a long cycle of self-betrayal. Trauma made me believe that my voice didn't matter, that my discomfort wasn't enough of a reason to say "no," and that avoiding conflict was safer than standing up for myself.

That's the thing about early trauma – it opens the door for every other form of pain to follow, and no matter how hard you try to box it away, it always rears its ugly head. And not just in romantic relationships. It also makes you fear feeling powerless any time you have to speak up for your own best interests. There have been times in my adulthood when I could actually feel it happening. I'd be in situations where I knew I needed to say that I wasn't ok with what was being said or done to me, but fear would take over, and instead of saying something, I'd remain silent. As a result, I found myself stuck in toxic relationships, both personal and professional, because I didn't have the courage to stand up for myself and walk away.

In therapy, I realized that the abuse had caused me to give my voice away. Not because I'd been cajoled into doing harmful things that were beyond my comprehension, but because I'd not allowed myself to acknowledge or discuss what had happened to me.

Believe it or not, I'd pushed the memory so far out of my mind that it didn't even surface when I was writing the first draft of this memoir. I'd been reviewing all the stories I'd already included, when – just like that – it all came rushing back to me. I couldn't believe it! I'd written an entire memoir about the dirty secrets I'd been carrying, and somehow, I forgot the biggest one of all – the one I've been holding onto for more than 45 years.

The secret that I'd been sexually abused as a child made space for every other secret I'd ever carry. It introduced my brain to the mechanism I'd use throughout my life to quiet the voice that would otherwise speak up in truth. Because I was so adamant that I was not a victim, I didn't heal properly from that trauma – even though I thought I had. I had always assumed that since I never lashed out, I was fine. I'd even successfully dealt with the flashbacks, by dissociating my emotions from the acts that took place. I truly believed that what was done to me didn't hurt me.

But I had been hurt. And while the abuse I'd experienced as a little girl had no visible effect on my life, it still affected me in many ways – most of which I was able to hide from everyone: family, friends – and me. The biggest thing was that it caused me to lose my voice. Not the public voice that would allow me to stand in front of crowds and speak or sing, but the one I'd need privately to say, "This relationship isn't working for me" or "What you did/said to me was hurtful" or "I don't want to do that."

It took decades and a complete breakdown to realize that I'd been carrying that little girl's pain around in a box marked "it doesn't matter." And because I'd never acknowledged it, I kept returning to the same patterns in every area of my life. I didn't know it, but I'd been re-creating my trauma over and over again, in situations where I felt small and powerless.

The Fact of The Matter

Certainly, not every woman has experienced sexual abuse or violence, but statistics suggest that over 53% of women have some form of sexual trauma in the fabric of their life's story. That means if it's not you who's endured abuse, you know someone who has. The numbers are staggering, but they point to why so many of us are fighting to get our voices back.

Whether abused or not, many of us experienced some form of trauma in our lives that hushed our voices. It made us ashamed that we didn't do more to help ourselves or that we didn't report our abuse to authority figures when we had the chance, and for many of us, the trauma still lingers, shaping our perceptions of ourselves and our place in the world. It whispers lies that make us think it's too late now to speak up about what we've experienced – or that if we do, we won't be believed, or – worse yet – no one will care. And so, we're convinced that our ability to keep quiet is proof that we're strong – that we've moved on.

But silence doesn't equate to strength. We are most powerful when we remove the "don't tell anybody" muzzles that were placed over our mouths – or which we placed there ourselves – and begin to speak openly about what we've been through. In order to reclaim the power that is rightfully ours we must refuse to hold on any longer to the residue of those secrets. Speaking up is an act of defiance against the trauma that wants to keep us silent. It's an assertion that we are no longer bound by shame or fear.

My silence wasn't my protector; it was my enslaver. It kept me tethered to my past, reliving the painful things that had happened to me. It stunted my growth, prevented me from healing, and wouldn't allow me to truly step into my power. The longer I remained captive, the more I believed that my voice didn't matter – that I didn't matter.

That's how I lost myself. That's how I lost the ability to advocate for the little girl who had been abused and to provide for her the healing she needed and deserved.

Even though I refused to be a victim, it was some time before I realized that I couldn't be a silent survivor, either. To remove the power the secret had over me meant I'd have to drag it into the light and speak about it. I had to give my survivor her voice back. She needed to be empowered to speak freely without shame and without guilt.

Break the Cycle

Burdens like these aren't ours to carry. They never were. But as long as we're silent, we continue to shoulder them. When we let those burdens go, we put them back where they belong – squarely on the shoulders of the ones who inflicted the trauma on us in the first place. To them belongs shame and the guilt – not us.

I no longer believe that I'm strong because I can pretend that the trauma and violence I've been through were no big deal. Hiding them only kept me from being aware of the real pain they were causing me, mentally and emotionally. I discovered that my strength was in my voice – in my ability to stand boldly in my truth. That strength empowered me to embrace, love, and respect myself – not despite what I'd been through, but because of it.

I went through the fire as a little girl, and I came out on the other side not even smelling like smoke. A warrior emerged from those flames. And while I hid her for many years, she's out now, and she's not afraid to be her unapologetically authentic self. She's no longer a victim, and she's more than a survivor – she's a conqueror.

SECRET 2

I Don't Think I'm Good Enough

I've asked myself a thousand times – what would "they" do if they knew I didn't want this life? That I'm strong because it's what I've always felt I had to be?

The truth is: I was taught to be strong. My father raised me to be self-sufficient, to dream big, and to go hard after my goals. The more I pursued, the more I was praised. He's coached me through tough challenges, and as a result, I have a relentless work ethic. My mother gifted me with her gentleness and the high standards of excellence for which she is known. Because of her, I learned very early how to handle people and situations with grace, love, and class.

What my parents got in return was a girl child who sought out and took on the most challenging tasks she could find, who staunchly held herself to her own impossible standards. I pushed myself hard. I wanted to be the best at everything – whether it was sports or my studies – I desired to be at the top. I always had high grades, and when I graduated from high school, I received the highest level of diploma one could earn. In college, I chose one of the toughest majors, and later, I earned not one, but two Master's degrees, followed by a doctorate.

Needless to say, I am the textbook definition of an overachiever.

From the outside, people probably assumed I was a naturally brilliant student, a young woman blessed with an innate drive for success. They saw the accolades, the certificates, the degrees – and thought it all came easy. But the reality was far from it.

I was emulating what I'd seen. Growing up, my parents made success look effortless. In fact, we kids had no idea what they were shouldering back then. We never saw them argue or complain about money; we never knew that they were struggling to hold things together. They shielded us from the harsh realities of life, and all we saw was their love, their hard work, and the way they always made sure our needs – and our wants – were met.

Make no mistake – our lives weren't perfect. My parents had their frustrations and their struggles. But no matter what happened, they handled it. And in the process, they taught me to do the same.

Somehow, though, I came to believe that I had to handle everything on my own, no matter what came my way, and that showing any sign of struggle or asking for help was a weakness.

One of my dad's favorite lines to me is, "I have confidence in you, so handle your business." It became my life's guiding principle, convincing me that I could tackle any challenge thrown my way. But as well-intentioned as he was, my mind received it differently. I started to believe that if I couldn't handle my business, I'd lose his confidence – and the thought of letting him down was simply unacceptable.

The Early Seeds of Self-Doubt

The seeds of my need to overachieve were planted early on. From a young age, I was taught to see potential in myself, and the people around me – teachers, parents, mentors – nurtured all the potential I displayed. They wanted to see how far I could go and how much I could achieve. Every time I received praise, a thirst was created in my brain for more of it. I started seeking affirmation like it was water in the desert.

This display of potential landed me in kindergarten at age four – before the days of the age requirement to start kindergarten. Because I was enrolled early, I was younger than everyone else. To my parents, this was a proud testament of my intelligence. To me, it felt like I was constantly behind, and I couldn't catch up.

It was more than just grades. It was the other stuff that matters to a girl – the first boyfriend, the first period, the driver's license. My classmates hit those milestones a year before I did, and it felt like an eternity. I often wondered what they'd think if they knew I still had an entire year to go before I was able to have the experiences they did.

So, I lied. From middle school (or Jr. High, as it was called back then) until high school graduation, I lied about my age. In fact, the year I turned 14, I remember my friends signing a card congratulating me on turning 15. I never corrected them. It was easier to let them believe I was "normal" than to admit the truth and feel "less than".

Chasing Validation

That need to "keep up" fed the need to prove myself, even at my young age. I poured all my energy into academics, desperate to outshine everyone and everything. In fact, I taught myself algebra during a summer break in junior high. It felt amazing to master a subject that seemed to intimidate my peers (and their parents). I felt powerful.

Until I met geometry.

I struggled horribly with that class, which was new for me. I'd never struggled in my academics before. I spent many nights working through theorems and proofs, trying to will myself to understand a subject that just didn't make sense to me. By the end of the year, though, I'd beat it. I had mastered the subject so well that I was correcting my teacher's mistakes.

That victory was intoxicating, and it simply prepared me to chase the next one.

From then on, I made sure to choose the hardest classes, to overload myself with credits, and to graduate with the highest honors on my diploma. I wasn't just a student. I was a girl on a mission. And when I got to college? I leveled up.

My original plan was to major in accounting. Then, the movie Jurassic Park premiered, and I was hooked. I was completely enthralled with the concept, the idea that humans could recreate life that had long been extinct. I discovered the world of genetics sitting in a movie theater and decided then and there that I would not go into accounting. Instead, I'd become a molecular biology major, so I could study genetics.

The leap made perfect sense to me, and apparently no one was surprised. It was so "on brand" with my ongoing pursuit of astronomical goals, no one ever questioned my decision or asked me was I sure it was a move I wanted to make. Now, I'm not sure which of us really won during my junior year at Hampton University – me or organic chemistry – but I did emerge from the program successfully, with a molecular biology degree in hand.

The Mask of Pretending

When I graduated and started my first job, the cycle repeated itself. I was the youngest once again and feeling like I had something to prove. My first role was as a receptionist, but it didn't take long before my boss noticed that I could do more. Within a year, a new department and role had been created just for me. Suddenly, people much older than me were looking to me for guidance.

The need to prove myself, to excel no matter where I was, pushed me into leadership roles early on. At 26, I was managing a clinical research office and overseeing physicians who were nearly three times my age. But no matter how much I achieved, no matter how many goals I met, I couldn't shake the feeling that I hadn't yet made it – that I still wasn't good enough.

So, I did the only thing I knew how to do: I pushed harder.

Despite a lifetime of accomplishments, I still felt like I had something to prove – like I wasn't really as smart as I thought I was, or as intelligent as everyone else believed me to be. It wasn't enough to succeed; I had to outdo my own achievements. The goalpost wasn't moving on its own; it was me who kept moving it.

I wasn't driven by ambition alone – I was driven by fear. Fear that one misstep would unravel everything, fear that people would see me for what I thought I was:. Still, I figured if I could just keep achieving, keep exceeding expectations, then maybe – just maybe – I'd finally feel worthy.

But I never did. Each success was a "flash in the pan", a fleeting moment of satisfaction before I shifted the bar higher. My sense of identity was intertwined with constant achievement. It wasn't enough to be employed; I had to be in leadership. One degree wasn't enough; I needed four. I didn't feel like I was enough unless I was excelling and receiving praise. Without them, I felt like I had failed.

My achievements were the mask I hid behind. I figured if I kept piling on accolades, I'd finally fill the gaping hole inside me. But instead, that hole seemed to grow deeper and darker. I was an overachiever, yes, but not out of passion or purpose. I was driven by the desperate need to prove something to the world. Every accomplishment was a way of papering over the unspoken secret: I'll never be good enough.

The Cost of Perfectionism

Looking back now, I understand that my childhood desire to please the adults in my life led to a fear of failing. Instead of reflecting on my accomplishments with pride and joy, I'd put them in front of me as new hurdles to jump. It turned into a vicious cycle where success wasn't a source of joy, but a new challenge I had to overcome.

This cycle of self-sabotage drove me to perfectionism, a terrible motivator that pushed me to chase something I could never attain because it doesn't exist. Perfectionism has nothing to do with striving for excellence; it's all about fear. Mine came from the fear that if I made a mistake, I'd be exposed as someone who wasn't as smart or as competent as she appeared to be. I was afraid that people would find out that my achievements were just a façade for my insecurity.

Society reinforces this for high-achieving Black women, doesn't it? It tells us we must work twice as hard to be considered half as good as our counterparts. We're conditioned from childhood to strive for flawlessness because the perception of weakness can be weaponized against us. And so, we bear our burdens, and keep climbing the ladder of success, even though we know that once we get to the top, we'll still have to keep proving ourselves.

But here's the thing: the pursuit of perfection is a losing game. There's no finish line, no moment where we finally get to rest and say, "I've made it." It's an illusion that we continue to be fooled by, yet we continue to chase it.

Still, perfectionism had me second-guessing every decision and questioning every move. It would meet me in bed at night, and whisper in my ear reminders that I'd never be good enough, and that no matter what I did, someone would find fault. I was plagued with overthinking, immobilized with indecision, and driven to exhaustion simply because I was trying to measure up to an impossible standard.

And then, when I'd inevitably fall short of perfection, it wouldn't just be a setback. To me, it was a failure of character and confirmation of what I already believed.

You Really Can Care Too Much

Now, it's one thing to shoulder the weight of your own expectations and challenges, but when you throw in the weight of other people's problems, it can turn into a real mess. It's no secret that I am a fierce supporter of the people I love. Let's just say, I'm "that" friend. In fact, there's a running joke among my friends and family: If you ever get into TROUBLE trouble, call Rhonda.

Of course, it's said with a chuckle, but there's truth in it: I've been called the Olivia Pope of my circle. Much like the character from the popular TV series, *Scandal*, I'm the fixer. When things fall apart, when questions need answers, when chaos demands order, I'm the one they all turn to.

In fact, I once had a friend come to me in full panic mode – thinking his life was about to be completely derailed by a woman who claimed she was pregnant with his baby. She had approached him with "proof" – medical reports and sonogram pictures, and he was knee-deep in fear. So, he brought it all to me. I took a look at the sonogram, did a quick Google search, and found the exact same image online. Turns out, she'd downloaded it. The more I dug, the more I uncovered. This woman had fabricated test results, hospital records – everything. All in an attempt to get his attention (and his money).

And she definitely had his attention, because she was threatening to take her "evidence" to his wife. He'd tried reasoning with her; he even sent her some money to make her go away, but it didn't work. Instead, it fueled her fire, and she went after him even harder – fabricating conversations and threatening to send people to his home.

So, of course, as "the fixer", I found her, confronted her with all the "receipts", and she folded. She knew she'd been caught, and the extortion plot was immediately over. My friend's marriage and career were saved – not because I'm a miracle worker, but because I knew the right questions to ask, where to look, and, well, because I have a certain set of skills.

Now certainly, this might be the most extreme example of my ability to "fix" things, but it's far from the only one. Untangling chaotic situations is one of my superpowers. Whether it's exposing a scam, helping someone avoid legal trouble, or resolving personal catastrophes, it's become something of a personal trademark.

At first, being the problem solver felt good. In fact, it is the foundation of my career and my success as a consultant and coach. But, over time, my desire to help others became another unhealthy burden. I started to believe that solving other people's problems was entirely my responsibility. It stopped being rewarding to help someone find a solution – it became a crushing expectation. It was another area of my life where I felt I needed to overachieve and prove that I could fix not only my problems but everyone else's, too. I convinced myself that I had to know everything, that not having an answer would mean I'd let someone down. I started taking on everyone else's crises as if they were my own, never stopping to ask myself if they should be the ones handling them.

Truth be told, I've spent many sleepless nights thinking of ways out of problems that weren't mine. I've carried the weight of other people's "what ifs" and worried about results that I didn't have to live with. I had saddled myself with the emotional and mental burdens of the things they were going through, in addition to my own.

In my mind, I was being strong by carrying so much responsibility. But, in fact, I just didn't know how to set boundaries. I didn't know how to say no. And then, my self-worth became tied to how well I could juggle the expectations of everyone around me. The more I tried to please everyone else, the less I recognized myself.

Death by Self-Sacrifice

This pattern of overwhelm and self-sacrifice is one I see in so many of us, especially we who are taught from an early age to carry everyone else's weight. We're conditioned to be the backbone, the nurturer, the one who holds everything together without breaking a sweat. "Strong" Black women don't complain. We don't falter. We just keep moving forward, even when the cost is steep.

This issue doesn't discriminate by class or income. Believe it or not, there are millionaires and celebrities – A-listers whose names you'd recognize – who will tell you they struggle with perfectionism and feeling like they're enough. They've cloaked their insecurities in their accomplishments, so no one will notice that, inside, they feel nothing like the person we see on red carpets and in interviews. Despite being in the upper echelon of society, they still carry the shame of feeling inadequate. Day in and day out, these individuals hear how amazing they are from fans and critics alike, yet they still struggle to feel like they're good enough.

Here's the truth: our worst is often better than most people's best. Even when we think we're just "good," we are still exceptional. But the real challenge isn't in being great – it's in accepting that we're great. It's realizing that failure is not the result of a personal flaw, that it's simply part of the journey. At times, it can be so hard to remember that we're not defined by our mistakes; we're made better by them.

It's often said that you can't pour from an empty cup, but let's be real – that's exactly what I was doing. Smacking the bottom of the bottle and giving away whatever happened to drip out. And when I inevitably couldn't provide as much as I wanted, at the level I wanted, I took that as a personal failure. I felt like I had to keep achieving and giving, even when I had nothing left to give. It was a cruel cycle I was putting myself through -- showing up exhausted, convinced that "being there" was better than not showing up at all.

Then, to add insult to injury, I'd then internalize my exhaustion. Instead of recognizing that I'd reached a limit, I'd criticize myself for not being able to do more. I'd convinced myself that not functioning at 100% all the time, for everyone, meant something was wrong with me – when the truth was: I was tired!

So, I'd drag myself to meetings and events and other obligations – no matter how double- or triple- booked I was. I'd push through the fatigue, the stress, and even sickness, because I believed that being strong meant sacrificing myself for all the people who "needed me" and showing up for them with solutions and answers no matter what I was going through or how I felt.

But here's what I realized: **sacrifices die.**

There are definitely causes worth fighting for, but none of the burdens I was shouldering were worth giving my life. The things I was doing out of a sense of obligation or because no one else volunteered were certainly not worth my health or my peace.

I was giving myself those little pep talks before I'd go into places – you know the ones – where we're sitting in the car giving ourselves the last look in the mirror, willing ourselves the strength to go inside. They're not to boost our self-confidence; they're survival talks. We're coaching ourselves to hold it together, because as long as we do, everyone will keep thinking we're ok.

But I wasn't okay. I was dying a little each time I "pushed through" without reserving anything for myself. Each time I showed up, I had less to give. Even when I wanted to give more, I couldn't, because I was tapped out.

Some might say this is a self-esteem issue – that if I just said more positive things to myself, I'd believe I was good enough. But it was impossible; I was forcing myself to live up to standards that no one can meet. I was kicking footballs at goalposts that wouldn't stop moving, and instead of adjusting my expectations, I internalized every miss as a sign of personal failure, and I became angry with myself for being unable to predict where the goalposts would move next. It was so hard to see reality: nobody gets it right all the time – not even the people we admire.

A Recipe for Burnout

My feelings of inadequacy and the fear of disappointing others were connected. Together, they drove me to try and exceed everyone's expectations, including my own. I thought that because I was strong, I could take on more than my fair share and allow the fate of the world to rest on my shoulders. My sense of worth and worthiness was defined by my view of other people's assessment of my value, not by what they actually thought of me.

The more I gauged myself by what I assumed people expected of me, the more resentful, undervalued, and taken advantage of I felt. All because I believed that they wouldn't be happy with me unless I said yes and overdelivered. And so, not only did I say yes to things I should have declined, but I also involved myself in situations where I wasn't needed and stayed in relationships long past their expiration dates. I pushed right past all the red flags and warning signs my body was sending me, and I kept going – because I was terrified that someone would find out that I didn't measure up.

When I finally reached my breaking point, I looked around, wondering where all those people I was so afraid of disappointing had gone. And I discovered that most of them never knew how much I'd been carrying for them. They never expected me to shoulder their burdens. I did that to myself. It was my choice – rooted in a belief that I wasn't valuable unless I was fixing, helping, and saving someone else.

I truly believed that if I didn't show up for other people, it would make me a bad friend, a terrible daughter, and a disappointing leader. But the truth is, the only person I was letting down was myself. Sacrificing everything on the altar of other people's needs was not love – it was desperation. Desperation to be seen, to be valued, to be deemed worthy. But that's the cruelty of self-sacrifice: the more you give, the less you have for yourself.

And while you're pushing yourself to the brink, no one notices. They just assume that's what you do. They assume you're built to carry it all, and they expect that you will because you always do. That is, until one day, you're on the floor, crumbling under the weight of it all, and no one has any idea. Not because they don't care, but because you've trained them to believe you're invincible.

No More Chasing Validation

It took hitting rock bottom for me to finally realize that I wasn't showing up for myself the way I'd shown up for everyone else. I thought I was proving my worth to them, but I was actually destroying myself. The version of strength I'd developed – the one that said I had to constantly prove my value and bear everyone else's burdens – wasn't strength at all. It was a trap. And I'd fallen for it. I'd been so caught up in "doing", that I'd forgotten who I was –without the titles, roles, or responsibilities.

As I healed, I discovered that there were some old habits I needed to break, and some new standards I needed to set. I needed to reprioritize myself – and get rid of the belief that it's selfish to attend to my own needs. It's not.

I had to give myself permission to be released from the old script that says I'm only valuable if I'm producing at high levels, while silently suffering and sacrificing who I am. I had to come to the understanding that my worth isn't defined by what I can do, nor is my value tied to how many problems I've solved or people I've saved. Eventually, it dawned on me that I am valuable simply because I am.

SECRET 3

I'm Heartbroken

As a teen, I often wondered what marriage would be like, but I didn't know what it meant to truly want it until I met my daughter's father. It wasn't love at first sight, though. In fact, we used to joke about how rude he was to me the night we met. But because fried chicken makes everything better, we became friends over a bucket of KFC.

From then on, we were basically inseparable. Even after he left Hampton University (where I was), and went to another college, we still managed to spend every possible moment together. Our relationship was goofy and fun. We cracked jokes on each other constantly and routinely held conversations by movie quotes and WWE sayings alone. We were best friends who laughed more than we cried and played more than we fought.

So, when he proposed, I excitedly said yes, and started planning my princess wedding. I envisioned us standing in a local cathedral, in full wedding attire, joined by the same officiant who'd married my parents. At 23 and 25, we did exactly that, exchanging vows in front of a huge wedding party and a couple hundred guests.

We had big plans for our life together. We wanted to travel in addition to furthering our education and careers. And we set out to reach those goals. We earned our Master's degrees together with him finishing first and with me waddling behind at a close second.

By the time my last few classes came around, I was quite pregnant with my daughter, Maiyah. I learned that semester that traditional desks are not suited for a 7-months-pregnant woman. She came a few weeks earlier than planned – in July of 2001 – induced to protect her life and mine. Now, when I tell you that this little baby girl was every bit of perfect, believe me, she was. I didn't know love until her father held her up for me to see. Not because I was flooded with the mother-baby bonding hormone, but because my first thought was, *Oh God, I have an ugly baby.*

I'd been in labor with her for so long that her face had flattened, and all of her features were smashed. In those initial drug-induced moments, I thought, *I'll have to love her because this child is about to grow up challenged, looking like this.* Later, though, after the drugs had worn off, the nurses brought her back to me, and she was perfect. Her features had plumped, and she was the most beautiful thing I'd ever seen.

I was so excited about her and our little family. I had all the high hopes in the world – she'd be 100% breastfed, and I'd only feed her homemade organic foods. She'd attend the best schools and have the brightest opportunities. I wanted to show her the world.

I'd also hoped that she'd be the first of several children. It had always been my desire to have at least three kids. But I had my hands full with what I had – a new, colicky infant and post-partum depression. I had no idea what I was doing – thank God for her grandparents, who seemed to know exactly what to do when I didn't.

Needless to say, I was devastated when my marriage to her dad began to crumble. There were a number of root causes, all of which I thought would be fixable with counseling and prayer. I was wrong. After months of trying to make it work, we called it quits.

I often say that divorce is worse than death. At least when someone dies, you never see them again. In a divorce, you're forced to deal with the "ghost" of someone you loved over and over. Whether they've truly changed or not, the person you once cherished feels like a stranger. It's hard to heal when you have to interact with a source of your pain. It's like trying to mend a wound that keeps getting torn open.

I didn't know what true emotional pain was until I went through that season. My marriage was my life, and everything I envisioned for my future was tied to it. In my mind, we were a team, destined to spend our lives together.

In our breakup, I didn't just lose a partner; I lost the life I had envisioned for us, and I was faced with the loss of the family we were supposed to raise, the dreams we'd shared, and the future we were building. Without him, I felt completely lost.

At 27, I found myself signing divorce papers with a two-year-old on my hip, wondering how I'd gotten there. My new identity was "single mom," a title I'd avoided my entire life. I had absolutely no desire to be a single parent, but there I was, having to figure out how to raise my daughter, how to provide stability for her, and how to navigate co-parenting with a man who, in many ways, no longer existed in my life.

In Sickness and In Health

Ask any mom, and she'll agree: motherhood is the real "in sickness and in health" relationship. There's no break, no pause button. Whether you're emotionally shattered or physically exhausted, your child is still there, needing your love, your care, and your attention. So, I did what I had to do – I buried my pain, buried my anger, and put on a brave face.

I didn't allow myself to dwell on my family falling apart. I had a daughter to think about. She hadn't asked for split homes and shuffled weekends. She deserved peace, and I was determined to give her as much of it as I could. But in my determination to shield her from the chaos, I buried my own feelings so deep that I didn't acknowledge them myself. I pretended I was fine even though inside I was completely shattered.

What made it worse was the fact that I was completely unprepared for it. I didn't come from a family of broken homes. So, divorce was foreign to me – and ours was public. We were "goals" – the couple's couple. Our married friends had looked up to us; our unmarried friends had wanted to be like us. And then, it was over, and everyone knew – our church, our family, our friends. Everyone.

Inside, I was very much not ok. I didn't want to be seen as a failure. So, publicly, I bounced back quickly. I faked a healing process that I never actually went through.

It took 15 years to heal from that divorce, because I refused to acknowledge my pain. I didn't want my hurt feelings to interfere with my daughter's relationship with her father. I knew she deserved that connection, and I wasn't going to be the one to sever it. So, I swallowed my anger and buried my resentment, even when I felt like I was being treated unfairly.

But there was a cost to that. In pushing down my emotions, I delayed my own healing. Every time I felt the sting of unfairness or had to force myself to play nice for her sake, the wound reopened, deeper each time. Even after I healed from the pain of the breakup, I carried the scars.

That heartbreak shook my self-esteem to its core, and I started questioning my worth, wondering why, yet again, I wasn't enough to make the marriage work. Those doubts made me vulnerable, and I found myself walking into another toxic relationship.

I Became Prey

When I met my second husband, I was still carrying the wounds of my first divorce. He swooped in at a time when I was emotionally fragile, and he knew exactly what to say to make me feel wanted, appreciated, and needed. By the time I realized the danger I was in, it was too late.

We married because it was expected of us. I was the pastor's daughter, singing on the ministry platform every week, and he was in a leadership position in the church. The fact that we were "shackin' up" was a scandal waiting to happen. We had tried to keep our living situation a secret, but it wasn't long before people started putting two and two together.

I'll never forget standing there during the ceremony, exchanging vows in my parents' home, and thinking, "It only cost me $750 to get divorced before. I can probably use the same lawyers this time, too." Certainly, that should have been my signal to run, but I didn't.

The marriage was miserable from day one. It was clear that I was in over my head, trying to manage a toxic relationship while hiding the truth from my family. I didn't want to let anyone know how bad things had gotten, and I certainly didn't want to admit that I had made a terrible mistake by marrying him in the first place. So, I pretended everything was ok – just as I had with everything else.

But this time, the stakes were much higher. I wasn't just dealing with emotional pain. I was living in fear for my life. There were nights when I genuinely believed my life was in danger. But it wasn't until the night he frightened my daughter that I found the strength to leave. That was enough. As she and I cowered together in her room, hiding behind the locked door he was trying to kick down, I knew I had to get out. The very next day, I packed up everything I could fit in my truck, and I left.

I Lost It All

When it was time to tell my family the truth of what happened between my ex and me, it was all I could do to form the words. My father wept. None of them had any idea that I was being abused.

I hadn't told them because I was afraid – scared of how they'd react, or that I'd be judged for staying as long as I had. I felt stupid for letting myself get trapped in such a destructive relationship. But the deeper fear was that if I told them, my father and brothers would end up in prison for what they'd do to him. And I couldn't handle that guilt, too, so I stayed quiet.

Leaving hadn't been easy. In fact, it was one of the hardest things I've had to do. In walking away from that marriage, I walked away from my first home, too – the one that had *my* name on it, no one else's. Things were so toxic, I had come to the conclusion that if I stayed, one of us was going to die and the other was going to prison. The only thing that was unclear was which of us it would be. To save both our lives, I walked away – from my home and nearly everything that was inside it. Eventually, the bank foreclosed on the property. I had officially lost it all. The despair was overwhelming.

For the next seven years, I lived with my parents, trying to recover from the emotional and physical trauma of that relationship. But instead of seeking therapy or support, I turned to destructive behaviors – drugs, alcohol, sex – anything that could help me forget the amount of pain I was in. I was trying to forget that I had let someone like that into my life. I wanted to drown out the memories and erase the mistakes I had made. So, by day, I was the consummate professional, climbing the leadership ladder, but by night, I lived dangerously, doing everything I felt big, bad, and brave enough to try.

Eventually, I realized that I was spiraling, and something had to change. I started going back to church, and when God gave me a clean slate, I took it. I told myself, "That second marriage never happened," and I repeated that mantra until it felt true. I'd boxed up yet another pain and buried it deep, adding it to the other scars I carried.

At Least I Have Friends... Right?

After two failed marriages, I concluded that perhaps romantic relationships weren't for me, and I chose instead to lean into platonic friendships. During my second marriage, I didn't have friends. Not only did my ex-husband frown upon any relationship I had outside of our marriage, I also couldn't risk having someone get close enough to me to find out the truth. So, I was starting from zero. It felt strange at first – going from no friends at all to having a social life, but I enjoyed having a sense of sisterhood and camaraderie. I thought I'd finally found people I could be myself with.

For a while, that seemed to be true – and then a pattern emerged: As soon as I'd allow my guard down and allow myself to be truly honest and vulnerable, those friends would disappear. I'd be completely bewildered, wondering what I'd done that caused them to walk away from our friendship, but most times, there were no concrete answers. Other times, I was told that I was just "too much".

I didn't know how to take that. I didn't know how I could be there for every single one of their low moments, but mine were "too much" for them. Those losses didn't just hurt – they were devastating. Perhaps even more than my divorces. I honestly thought that I was building relationships that would last a lifetime, and instead I'd found myself blindsided by abandonment.

These women weren't just associates; they were sister-friends I'd loved and had poured my heart into. We knew each other's secrets, had shared in victories, and had cried together. In many ways, we were family. So, to have them exit my heart with little to no warning left me completely shattered once again.

At the time of my breakdown, I was mourning the loss of someone I considered to be my best friend. The feelings of abandonment and rejection from that loss stung more than any romantic breakup I ever had. One week we were the best of friends – the next we were estranged. For months, it was all I could think about. I couldn't sleep and my brain was cluttered with thoughts of our final conversation. I replayed it over and over, wondering how things could have gone so wrong and why I couldn't fix it. I questioned everything -- about myself and about my value as a friend.

That breakup broke me in a way I never could have anticipated, and the loss weighed on me heavily. Once again, I found myself asking, "What's wrong with me?"

No one talks about how losing a friendship can hurt the same way a breakup with a boyfriend or girlfriend can. When you lose a friendship, you don't just disconnect from someone you love, you lose a major part of the rhythm of your life: inside jokes, daily routines, shared experiences, favorite places – they're no more.

It's quite disorienting, really – to lose someone you loved deeply, but to know they're not truly gone, they're just no longer a part of your life. It left me with a lot of self-doubt, and it shot my sense of self-worth out of the water. This wasn't the first friendship that had ended abruptly and unexpectedly. There were others, and in my mind, there was only one common denominator – me.

I started to believe that I needed to guard myself against friendships, now, too, because I couldn't take the risk of getting close to someone else and losing them once they found out that I was "too much". I accepted that I wasn't suitable for close friendships, and even though I longed for them, I had to protect myself and I had to protect anyone who believed they wanted to befriend me. I had to make sure that neither of us ended up damaged by "the real" me.

All In My Business

So, I turned to what I felt I had left – my business. This was where I felt comfortable – where I knew I could pour in my entire heart and get a return. I figured there was no way an inanimate object could hurt me the way people had, and so I jumped into it with both feet. I'd been coaching business owners and entrepreneurs for a while, helping them to get good results when it came to launching and growing, but I didn't feel I was making an impact at the level I truly desired. There were so many Black women connected to me who needed support – the kind only fellow entrepreneurs understand – so I decided to start a support and coaching group to fill that need.

EntrHERpreneur was a community aimed at supporting women entrepreneurs who were navigating the ups and downs of building their businesses. I spent hours curating content, organizing events, and building a community that proved to be a safe haven for many women. The movement was so important to me, I wrote my first book about it, with the same name. EntrHERpreneur wasn't just a business; it was an extension of me and a part of my purpose.

The group started with just seven women meeting for brunch, and it grew exponentially. Soon, we had more than fifty women regularly attending our events, sharing their wins and struggles, and supporting each other's growth. I had big plans for it. I envisioned us expanding nationwide, hosting conferences, and launching mentorship programs. To me, the possibilities seemed endless.

So, when I decided to trademark the name, I thought I was taking a step to protect what I'd built. Little did I know that this decision would awaken a corporate giant who had attorneys on standby waiting to pounce on anyone using the word "entrepreneur" in specific categories of their trademark application. They saw my little business as a threat and came after me with guns blazing. Before I knew it, I was embroiled in a legal battle that I clearly couldn't win. They wanted me to take down everything connected to the name – my website, my book – everything.

I was crushed. I had prayed for that name. God had given me EntrHERpreneur. So why would He let it be taken away? Why would He let something that had brought so much joy and fulfillment to me and the women in my community be snatched out of my hands?

When God finally answered, His response was clear and painful: "Because I'm through with that."

I was floored. We were just getting started! How could He be through with it? It seemed completely unfair. I had already lost so much in my personal life; I needed this win. I needed to believe that I could be part of something successful, that I could build something that would last. But the answer didn't change, and I had no choice but to let it go. I deactivated the website, took down all my branded materials, and tried to move forward. But I couldn't. My heart was still tethered to the dream.

I tried to hold on to the brunches, at least, but then the Covid pandemic hit, and I had to stop those, too. None of the re-branding ideas I came up with worked. I'd given up EntrHERpreneur as a name, but I wasn't ready to let go of the business. I just couldn't let it go. I continued trying to resuscitate a brand God had clearly pronounced dead. And of course, it never came back to life.

I finally let it go and decided to move on to another area of coaching. By then, I'd coached a few clients to write books, and I decided to lean further into author coaching. I had some success, but still, I couldn't seem to put my heart into it fully. As a result, the program wasn't taking off the way I had hoped it would. Baffled by this, I talked with my business coach, and she hit me with a painful truth: "You haven't grieved the death of your business."

And that was it. It was like the lights had come on and I could see the rubble of my business all around me. She was absolutely right – I had been angry, but I hadn't grieved. I hadn't acknowledged the loss; I had just buried it and moved on, like I had done with every other heartbreak in my life. It wasn't until that moment that I allowed myself to feel and express the hurt I felt, and it rushed in like a flood.

Grief Is a Journey You Can't Fake

With so many losses, I wondered if I was permanently broken – like, maybe my heart just wasn't meant to be whole. It seemed like every time I was close to healing, I'd be dealt another blow, and my heart would be shattered all over again. So, I locked it away and hid the pain I was carrying from rejection and abandonment. It was the only way I knew to protect myself and to make sure no one ever discovered that a friendship with me was doomed because I was unlovable. On the surface it worked – There were plenty of people I was friendly with, but very few who were real friends.

Healing from a broken heart might just be the hardest thing I've ever had to do. It comes in stages, but those stages aren't linear. You'll take two steps forward, and a memory, a smell, or a song will remind you of the person or place you're missing, and suddenly grief will snatch you four steps back. Time might take the edge off of grief, but even years later, there might still be an ache. Some days, the pain might hit you full-force and unexpectedly, and snap you back to the memories, like they just happened yesterday.

We've all experienced grief on some level, but none of us knows exactly how we will grieve a loss or for how long. It's an intensely personal journey that most of us don't give ourselves enough time to navigate. We're so quick to push through the pain of loss, hoping that it will just go away or that we'll forget about it.

The (not so) funny thing about grief is that you can push past it for a time, but at some point, it's going to come up, tap you on the shoulder, and remind you that it hasn't gone anywhere. And it usually happens at the most unforeseen and inconvenient times, leaving you to wonder why you exploded in anger or burst into tears from seemingly nowhere.

I didn't realize that there were things happening in my life that added to the brokenness of my heart. And it wasn't just the major, life-defining moments. Every time I felt overlooked, forgotten, or betrayed, little pieces of my heart were being chipped away. Of course, because they seemed insignificant to me, I never felt a need to address my hurt or heal from them. I figured, as a strong Black woman, I simply needed to suck it up and keep moving forward.

When it came to the major heartbreaks – the breakups and the failures – I bypassed the process of healing because I didn't want to give power to the people who'd hurt me. I felt as though my grief gave them too much attention. I chose revenge over wholeness. I tried to numb myself to them and the hurt they caused, rather than sit with the truth of my feelings, so I could heal and forgive.

Instead of being honest with myself about the depth of my pain, I continued showing up – in the spaces I'd been hurt and around the people who'd hurt me – pretending that I was ok. I'd told myself that one day, I'd actually be as unbothered and happy on the inside as I was trying to look on the outside. But to get there, I'd have to learn to tolerate this pain. So, I subjected myself to the reminders of all the ways I'd been hurt over and over again and deemed myself successful if I didn't cry or have a panic attack immediately afterward.

And eventually I didn't. But ultimately, this extremely toxic version of "exposure therapy" caught up with me.

I didn't know it, but I was abusing myself. I was repeatedly reinjuring myself and not allowing any time to heal. It was equivalent to going to the hospital for a stab wound, getting stitched up, and then ripping the stitches out – on purpose.

You Can't Just "Move On"

Quite a lot of us are walking around with smiles on our faces and broken hearts. We've attempted to move on from life-altering pain without acknowledging that we're still hurting. It's like someone stomped on our foot, and rather than yelling, "Ouch!", we chose to smile and limp on.

That unresolved pain now impacts how we see and interact with the world. We've become skeptics who don't believe in the genuineness of people anymore. And so, we implement a "trust tax", appropriately named by business-strategy guru Dr. Sam Chand. It's the way we make new people pay for the way the old people hurt us, because we believe that if someone we love could do [that thing] to us, then everyone else will too.

So, we make the new people jump through hoops to prove they're different. In dating, we set impossible standards. In friendships, we keep things at surface-level, never letting anyone get too close. In business, we tighten our policies and grow suspicious of customers and colleagues. We wear our skepticism like badges of honor, pretending we're operating from positions of strength, intentionality, and discernment, when the truth is we're operating out of fear.

We ultimately spend our lives warding off what we don't want, instead of living them in affirmation of what we do want. Instead of giving people the opportunity to offer us their best, we instantly assume the worst of them. We live by the words "NEVER AGAIN," and we guard ourselves against the possibility of further pain.

We've convinced ourselves that forgetting is the same thing as healing – that as long as we're not thinking about the person who hurt us or that painful situation, we're fine. But we're not. All we did was adjust to the pain until it became background noise we didn't hear anymore. It's the same as with physical pain; when you live with an ache long enough, eventually, your brain learns to tune it out.

But, forgotten pain doesn't equate to healing.

It's no secret that rejection, abandonment, and heartbreak can be devastating. The pain can hurt like hell. I came to see that the only way I could truly move past them was to be honest about how I felt and to actually go through the process of healing – and forgiving. I couldn't keep pretending to be strong by carrying pain and grief around forever.

The truth is: I've lost things and people I'll never get back. And I realize that the pain from those losses may never completely go away. But I also know that grief and despair can't be in the driver's seat. They cannot have permission to continue standing between me and the life I desire. I'd have to heal if I wanted any chance at receiving the love, joy, and fulfillment I was seeking. There was just no way to get around it.

SECRET 4

I'm Pretty Sure God's Forgotten About Me

Believe it or not I've always struggled with my faith. I'm not sure if all PK's (Preacher's Kids) have this issue, but I had a hard time believing that all the stuff they said about God pertained to me. I had no problem believing that He loved and helped others. I had seen what He had done for them, but it took a long time for me to believe that I was included. Nevertheless, I tried to believe. I tried to "have faith", because it was the thing they always told us to do.

I had no problem believing that God is real, even with a strong background in the sciences. I've always believed that the beauty, wonder, and complexity of life and nature were crafted by His design. But having faith – real, unshakable faith that worked when I needed it – was something else entirely. Faith didn't seem to operate for me the way it did for everyone else, so I began to think that maybe I wasn't doing it right, or maybe I just didn't qualify.

Now, I am the definition of a true church baby. My aunt made my first choir robe – because apparently robe makers don't design for two-year olds. From that young age, I was always active in church. My parents made sure that I was involved in everything that was created for a child in church – including those dreaded Easter recitations, where every child had to learn a scripture or a part in the Easter play. From singing in the children's choir to running the administrative office, when it comes to church, I've done it all.

With all that church exposure, you'd think my faith would have been rock-solid. By the time I hit young adulthood, I should've been the one "speaking to the mountains" and watching them move. But I wasn't. I'd only mastered the art of looking and sounding like a good church girl. I could sing the songs and speak the lingo. But it was all surface – nothing more than a shiny, polished exterior. I never felt that deep, soul-changing connection that other people claimed to have. I'd watch as others seemed to have their lives transformed, while I went home from church every Sunday feeling just as empty as I'd arrived – if not more.

I didn't understand how to make the transition from what I saw to what I experienced. I thought that believing in God made everything better. But, as a young adult whose marriage was falling apart, I couldn't reconcile what I was supposed to believe and what was happening in real time. I had done everything I thought I was supposed to do – praying, fasting, counseling, believing for a miracle. But none of it seemed to matter. The more I pleaded for God to save my marriage, the more distant He seemed.

It felt like I was trying to knit a rope on one end that that kept unraveling at the other. I was frustrated, and it seemed that my faith wasn't working. Here I was, with a toddler, no job, and a broken heart trying to make myself understand how a God who loved me could let such a terrible thing happen to me. I really tried to see Him in it all, but I just couldn't. Everything I'd ever believed about faith and prayer being able to change things was failing right in front of me.

I wasn't able to see it at the time, but in the middle of my first divorce, despite all my floundering and complaining, God sent a glimmer of hope to me. While I was stressing about whether I'd be able to close on the townhome my ex and I had been planning to purchase, He directed me one Saturday afternoon to reach out to a new mortgage broker, who just happened to be in his office that morning and returned my inquiry message in minutes. We talked for a while, and then he did something I didn't expect – he prayed for me, right there on the phone, and told me to come into his office that Monday so he could help me close the deal by myself. In that brief moment, I felt something shift. It wasn't a full-on breakthrough, but it was enough to keep me from falling completely off the edge. It was a reminder that maybe – just maybe – God hadn't forgotten about me after all.

That helped me hang on a little while longer. But years later, after my second marriage ended, the outcome was different.

I'd spent the entire marriage pretending to be part of a praying power couple – an image that I desperately hoped we'd become. Because we both held leadership positions in our church, we never let on to what was going on at home, behind the scenes. In public, we appeared to have a strong, faith-filled partnership. But behind closed doors, it was chaos. I was miserable and desperately hoping that God would swoop in and transform our mess into a ministry.

He didn't.

Instead, I had to endure another traumatic breakup and by the time that was over, I was done with God. I turned my back on him and wanted nothing to do with him. I had come to the conclusion that He didn't care about me and rather than helping me to build my faith in him, He was allowing things to happen that just made it harder. I felt like I couldn't trust Him with my heart anymore. What hurt the worst was feeling like so many others had turned their backs on me, and God – the one person who was never supposed to leave or forsake me – seemed to have done just that.

For years I carried the dirty secret that I was a church girl – a PK – who didn't believe. Who couldn't believe. But I couldn't disgrace my family by completely walking away. So, I pretended to be someone I wasn't. Even though I was still going to church, I was living a Godless life. I forced myself to go to church each week, but while there, I'd spend all my time hiding in the church's office doing administrative work. It was the only way I could satisfy everyone's expectations that I'd be there, even though I had no desire to participate.

Lashing out with destructive behavior was my way of telling God that I didn't need him – that if he'd forgotten about me, I could forget about him too. And so, I turned toward substances and people to help me forget. I was actively trying to become addicted to something – anything. I figured it would distract me from the pain I was in, and it would help me forget about how abandoned I felt.

It's only in hindsight that I see just how much of God's grace was covering me. There were nights I shouldn't have made it home. Days I should've lost my mind. But somehow, I didn't. I didn't realize what I was doing to myself or the danger I was putting myself in, and quite honestly, at the time, I didn't care. Yet, I was kept. And I know now that it was the relentless prayers of my parents and God's refusal to let me go that kept me alive and unaddicted.

As I began contemplating turning my life around, God began beckoning me to return to him. It's funny how He works that way. Even when I was running full speed in the opposite direction, He was orchestrating my return to Him. Of course, I initially had no interest. I didn't want to go back to pretending that there was something between God and me that wasn't. But He made it so that I couldn't avoid it. Nearly everywhere I'd go to socialize, I'd run into people from a church I'd never heard of. It seemed like every restaurant and event I went to with friends, I'd be introduced to someone from Mount Lebanon Missionary Baptist Church, affectionately known as "The Mount."

If you have heard the saying that God will meet you where you are, I can confirm that to be true. I met most of the people I'd later love like family outside the four walls of that church. Their love for each other and their invitations sparked me to check them out one Sunday. Walking through the door was very much like walking into a strange, but familiar place. It looked and sounded like the kind of church I was used to, but there was a difference. It wasn't like before, when it seemed like the Word was for everyone else in the room, except me. This time, it felt like the pastor, Bishop Kim Brown, was talking directly to me. It was like he knew me, and it was just the two of us in the sanctuary. It didn't take long for me to learn to bring a pen and notebook, and to wear waterproof mascara to church on Sunday mornings. I left every service a mess – with makeup smeared, eyes swollen, and heart changed.

Those early days of returning to church were filled with longing and fear. I loved being in God's presence, but I was afraid of what would happen if I opened my heart back up to Him again. I didn't want to admit to myself that deep down I was hoping for something – a breakthrough or some sort of sign that God still saw me and cared. So, I would sit in the back during service and rush out as soon as it was over. I didn't want anyone to notice me. I wasn't ready to be welcomed, to make connections, or engage in small talk, because I wasn't even sure that church was where I wanted to be.

In fact, I didn't tell my parents that I'd started going back to church. I hid that I was sneaking there on Wednesday nights and early Sunday mornings, because I wasn't ready for them to know I was changing – that God was calling me. I wasn't ready to admit that I had been lashing out on purpose, out of a hatred toward God. I didn't want to get their hopes up that I'd be coming back to church and resuming the church life I'd left. I knew I didn't want that. If I was to return, I knew I needed something more, something deeper, than functioning in church. If God and I were going to have anything, we'd have a true connection first.

Then I started to wonder how my parents would feel about embarking on this journey at a different church. I'd only ever been a part of their ministry, and I feared that attending a different one would be hurtful to them and would negatively impact our relationship. But I couldn't shake this desire. So, I continued to sneak off to church each week.

I decided to come clean about my whereabouts on New Year's Eve 2013. I felt ready to embark on a new walk with God, and I was tired of hiding it. I wanted to start 2014 off with a new commitment, and so I told my parents where I'd been disappearing off to during the week. And as I should have known all along, they weren't hurt; they were happy that I was finally coming back into the fold. Their prayers were answered.

The Road to Restoration

The road to rebuilding my relationship with God wasn't an easy one. I wanted to believe that He loved me, that He hadn't forgotten about me. But years of pain and disappointment had built up walls around my heart. I was guarded, wary of getting my hopes up only to have them shattered again. The hardest part was believing that I was worthy of His love and attention. I had spent many years thinking I wasn't good enough for Him to love me, and that I hadn't done enough to deserve His favor. I thought that every bad thing that had happened to me was His way of punishing me for my failures and my inability to believe.

I had to shed those misconceptions and misunderstandings about God and get to know him for myself; I did a lot of unlearning. I had to confront the bitterness and anger I'd harbored against Him for so long. I had to shed the idea that God's love was conditional – that it was based on how "good" I was or how perfectly I performed. And in the setting down of those old ideas, I started to realize just how much I was loved by God. Even when I hated Him, He sent reminders that let me know He hadn't forgotten about me. In fact, He had allowed me to leave His side and wander for a bit, but eventually, He came and found me. And when He called, thankfully, I had the presence of mind to answer, "Here I am".

Even though I rededicated my life to Christ, I still struggled to believe that He was there for me. That struggle was a large part of the breakdown I experienced. While my life was in the chaos of responsibilities, work, community, family and more, I expected Him to do something. I wanted Him to come to my rescue. I wanted that big, "Ten Commandments" voice booming down from heaven, saying, "My child…" But I didn't get that. Instead, the night I broke down, I was snapped back to the time when

I was bitter and hateful toward Him. He'd let me down again. He'd left me to hit rock bottom and didn't even bother coming to find me.

It felt like the end of everything. I was on the floor, sobbing, screaming at God, feeling completely forsaken. I'd done all the "right" things – again – and still ended up broken and defeated. It was as if everything I'd been working to rebuild over the last decade had crumbled right under my feet.

Those old thoughts started resurfacing and I started to wonder if I had made a mistake in recommitting myself to Him because, once again, when I felt I needed Him most, He was silent. If He really loved me, He would have miraculously stepped in and fixed it all. It didn't make sense to me that I could be doing so much for everyone – going above and beyond their expectations – yet still feeling like it didn't matter to them – or to Him.

As I lay on the floor crying out to Him that night, I was angry, and I felt hopeless. How could I allow myself to get back to this point? What use is it to live for God, if when you *really* need Hin, He's going to feel furthest away? What was the point of being on this journey if – when it really mattered – all I could expect was abandonment and disappointment? How could I believe that Jesus will work it out if nothing is, in fact, working out?

I Had It All Wrong

During my time of healing, I learned that my perception of God was skewed and that my faith needed to be shifted. It was easy to become resentful toward God because He wasn't acting in the way I wanted Him to, at the speed I wanted Him to, because I thought He wasn't speaking to me. Thing is, he'd already spoken. I just hadn't been listening.

The entire time leading up to my breakdown, God had been trying to get me to rest – to take some time off to reprioritize my life and attend to my mental and physical health. I was so stressed out, I'd gained 40 pounds, was having unexplained heart issues, and had become diabetic. I knew I was taking care of everyone except me. And when I'd feel the nudge to rest, I'd tell friends and family that I was going to take a few days to disconnect from work, but I'd always find a reason to end up back at my desk. It was like my computer was the drug and my offices were trap houses. I couldn't seem to step away from giving all I had to all the roles I was playing, even though I didn't have anything more – physically, mentally, or emotionally – to give any of those places.

So, when I found myself at what some might consider a "curse God and die" moment, I wanted Him to speak then and rescue me in real time. The truth was He had been speaking the entire time, trying to prevent me from getting to where I'd ended up. It was like he'd been watching His toddler throw a tantrum over candy she couldn't have – even though there was plenty already in the grocery cart.

For months, I'd been burning myself out – yet piling on more responsibilities. I was exhausted, but I had convinced myself that if I didn't personally do all the things that needed to be done, the whole world would come crashing down around me.

God had indeed spoken to me, and His word was *rest*. Not the kind of rest you get by simply going to bed earlier or taking a nap during the day – He was telling me to let go. He knew what was coming, so there was no new word and no new direction to be given, because He knew I didn't have the capacity to take on one iota of another thing. He was trying to protect me from myself.

Ah! Now I Get It

There are myriad ways God was showing me His love, but they were rarely the grand, dramatic gestures I was expecting. I was looking for Him in the form of a big miracle or a "sky-opening" moment, forgetting that sometimes His love is expressed in the small, subtle nudges I received every day. But I was overlooking them because I was so focused on looking for what I wanted to find.

I discovered that my love for God and my faith in Him couldn't be dependent upon some grand display of His power or receiving an immediate solution to all my problems. I had to learn to recognize the small, consistent ways He works. And even more, I had to know for myself, deep down, that He truly cares, even when it feels like everything is falling apart.

I also had to remember that God doesn't operate on my timeline or in the ways I might choose. He's not absent; He's intentional. He sees the bigger picture and loves us enough to let some things fall apart so better things can come together. Each disappointment, each detour, wasn't a sign of His neglect, but of His deep, abiding love. Every time I thought I'd hit a dead end, He was setting me up to take a new direction. I discovered that even when things didn't feel good, He was working them together for my good.

That realization opened the doors for my faith to be strengthened and deepened. I began rebuilding a walk with God that isn't dependent on getting what I want, when I want it, but faith that trusts His character even when I don't understand His plans. That's what real faith is – trusting Him, not just for what He can do, but for who He is. It's knowing that even when the path ahead is unclear, He is the One who is guiding. He sees us, He loves us, and He is never absent from our struggles.

This journey of rediscovering God's love didn't just restore my hope; it empowered me to approach life with a new kind of strength. I no longer need to carry the weight of trying to force things into place, trying to "fix" my life on my own. Instead, I can rest in the assurance that I am deeply cared for and that He knows His plans for me, and they are good – even if they don't always make sense in the moment.

The beauty of this revelation is in the understanding that I don't have to perform my way into God's acceptance. I'm no longer striving to prove that I'm worthy of His love. I am loved, simply because I am His. And that realization is humbling because it means I don't have to fight for a place at His table; He's already prepared one for me. I don't have to exhaust myself trying to be "good enough" for Him. He made me – beautifully and wonderfully – and called me "good".

And that is enough.

SECRET 5

It's All on Me

I don't think what we're experiencing these days is what Chaka Khan and Whitney had in mind when they belted out,

"I'm every woman… It's all in meeeee
Anything you want done baby – I do it naturally."

Honestly, I'll naturally do more than I should – probably way more and perhaps too much. For so long, "doing it all" has been glamorized, to the extent that we really think we're supposed to be every woman and that it really is supposed to be all on us.

Over the years, we've had songs and movies make us believe that we are the glue that holds it all together. We are the ones who make sure the family stays connected and that everyone gets everything they need. We're groomed to do the mental and emotional heavy lifting for everyone around us – so much so, that the people around us barely have to think for themselves. We do all the thinking for them.

If someone asked for my help, I rarely declined – even if knew I didn't have the time or the resources, I'd say yes anyway. I'd take on projects and roles that I had no business accepting, jobs I had no capacity for, and responsibilities I didn't want. I became the woman who couldn't sit still or set boundaries. Even when my calendar was crammed beyond recognition and my physical and mental health were deteriorating, I didn't stop. I didn't know how to stop. In my mind, I was being helpful, but in reality, I was self-destructing.

Looking back, this is how I ended up in an advisory role at an organization that was already a sinking ship. It didn't take me long to figure out that I had gotten in over my head. The problems they were facing were far beyond what one person could solve. Still, I convinced myself that I could fix it. If it could be done, I could do it. I had to. I had been recommended for the post by someone I deeply respected, and I didn't want to let them down.

So, I stayed in the role, becoming more and more entangled in the day-to-day operations, until I was no longer just advising, but involved in full-time oversight. I tried to manage it all while still holding down my own businesses full-time, still serving my clients, still being present for my family, and still fulfilling my obligations at church and in the community.

When the leadership environment became hostile, I found myself struggling with the guilt of even thinking about leaving. *Would I be disappointing my team? Would they see me as a quitter?* Despite knowing that I had done far more than my fair share, I still felt shame for having to admit that I couldn't succeed in such a toxic space. And yet, the thought of staying filled me with resentment and anger. I felt trapped, torn between my sense of obligation and my own deteriorating well-being.

By the time of my breakdown, I was working ridiculous hours trying to keep up with the demands of everything I'd obligated myself to. I knew I'd taken on too much, yet I couldn't let anything go. It felt like if I loosened my grip even a little, everything would collapse. I was literally in my office from early morning until long after midnight, only getting up for bathroom breaks. I was working through meals, cheating myself of sleep, and neglecting my own needs. My body was running on fumes.

When I finally walked away from that role, I was physically, emotionally, and mentally depleted. I'd completely lost sight of my own needs, my own boundaries, and my own health. All because I believed it was completely on me to make it work.

It Was a Circus, but I Wasn't Having Fun

While all this was happening, I still had a million things going on at home and beyond. I had to keep up with all the moving pieces of my own businesses and family, stay on top of everyone's needs and schedules, anticipate problems before they arose, and somehow keep everything running smoothly. There was literally no off switch.

I had to ask myself, is this really the life the lady in the Enjoli commercial was living back in the 80s, when she said she could bring home the bacon and fry it up in a pan? … 'Cause she's a woman?

If it is, I have questions.

The first one is – *Why would anyone aspire to this?*

Seriously, women – especially single moms – know there's no PTO for reality. Bills don't pause when you're tired or when you're sick. There's no one else to take the kids to practice, no one else to handle car repairs, no one to pick up the slack when you're running on empty. We don't get to hand off the responsibilities of parenting just because we need a break. We don't have the option to bow out when we're overwhelmed. If we don't show up, everything really does fall apart.

I was doing it all because I felt I had to, not because I wanted to. There was literally no one to delegate life's responsibilities to, and when it came to work obligations – I took those on because there was no one else who could do it correctly. I'd grown accustomed to the mindset that if something needed to be done, and there was no one to do it, then it was my responsibility to handle it. It just didn't seem acceptable to allow something to simply go undone.

To the outside world, it looked like I was expertly juggling all the things – which made me appear to be "strong," but no one truly saw the toll it was taking. They didn't see my frustration and overwhelm – the times I was busy until late at night, doing everything other than what was on my task list for the day. They didn't see my resentment or my exhaustion from having so many obligations every day and every weekend, with no end in sight.

They had no idea how much I wished I had help.

It's not like I'd never asked for help, nor is it that people never offered. I did ask, and people did offer, but when it was time for the rubber to meet the road, many times those folks didn't come through, or they only half-did what they promised. Some of them "helped" so horribly I still ended up doing the task after cleaning up the mess they'd made. So, I figured what's the use? I knew what needed to be done, and even if I didn't know how to execute it, I knew I could figure it out. Past experience had shown me that I'd end up spending the time anyway, so I just stopped asking. I stopped expecting adequate help or any help at all. I accepted that I am all I've got, that it really is on me to get things done, and I carried on.

But I'm Not Your Superwoman

Even in my relationships, it was hard to rely on a partner because I was afraid of being let down. Every time I was disappointed, it just reinforced the belief that I had to do it all. In fact, one of the reasons I became disinterested in pursuing romantic relationships was because I was afraid I'd be disappointed yet again by a significant other's forgetfulness, weaponized incompetence, or selfishness. So, I trained myself to be content in my singleness and convinced myself that I was ok with not needing or having a partner. It just seemed to be easier to do it all alone than to risk trusting someone and being let down.

The term for this behavior is called hyper-independence. It's when you choose to do everything on your own because you can't trust that others want to help – or worse, because you don't believe they will. It happens when you've been repeatedly forgotten, overlooked, gaslit, and disappointed, so you opt to do everything yourself because it feels safe.

Experts say hyper-independence is a trauma response, but unless you're a therapist (or in therapy), you may not easily recognize it as such. Those of us who behave this way use it as a shield to protect ourselves from rejection. It's our way of removing expectations for support and help, so there's no pain to feel when we don't receive them. And while it does keep us from having to depend on others, it also keeps us on the path of being overworked and overextended.

When people called me "strong" or "Superwoman," they meant it as a compliment, but they couldn't see my reality – that I was stuck under the weight of that. They didn't see how bitter and resentful I'd become, after being the go-to person for everyone else's problems, yet having no one to turn to for my own.

Being an entrepreneur on top of all that only quadrupled the weight. I don't know when it became sexy to be entrepreneur, but somewhere along the line someone started the myth that "being your own boss" as a business owner meant freedom. The truth is entrepreneurship is a different kind of pressure. Instead of being responsible for just your job role, you're responsible for everything – from generating revenue to meeting payroll to delivering services. One wrong move could set you back months, or even years. And when things go wrong – as they inevitably do – there's no manager to complain to or blame, because it's you.

Yes, I was the boss, but I was also the bookkeeper, the marketing department, the strategist, the designer, the CEO, the service provider, and more. Every move the business made, both good and bad, was on me. And while I certainly reveled in the triumphs, I also packed on more PTSD from the investments I made in people and services that ended up returning more losses than gains. So, when it was time to build the team I needed to help expand my business, it was incredibly hard to let go of control. I didn't want to make another damaging decision, and I didn't like feeling as though I was handing my helpless babies over to total strangers.

Truth Is, I'm Tired.

I was doing everything myself because I didn't trust anyone else to get it right – whether it was in my life or my business – I had a hard time believing that people would do what they'd promised, and if they did, they'd make me regret depending on them in the first place.

The truth, though? I was tired of holding everything together. I wanted help. I wanted someone to ask me how they could support me and actually follow through. But by the time I came to this realization, no one was offering. I had done such a good job of making it appear that I had everything all together and under control, no one ever noticed I was drowning.

It became obvious to me that I wasn't growing anymore – personally or professionally. My plate was so full that I couldn't take on anything new. I couldn't even think up new ideas because my thoughts were so consumed with my existing responsibilities. It hit me that my hyper-independence and my need for control weren't protecting me and allowing me to push forward; they were holding me back and keeping me stuck.

Turn It Off

I carried too much for too long and it affected every aspect of my life. I wasn't just tired; I was weary. I was constantly on the edge – like one more thing would send me spiraling out of control.

It wasn't the usual exhaustion – I was entirely depleted by the emotional, physical, and mental heavy lifting that I was doing day in and day out. It was the pressure of knowing that my livelihood and the livelihood of others depended on my decision making. It was the fear of letting people down and being seen as a failure. It was the weight of feeling like so many people were counting on me to succeed.

I showed up for them every day looking fierce and ready to take on the world, but I felt completely different inside. I was in a constant battle with myself, having to choose between everyone else's expectations and my own needs – and consistently denying mine and choosing theirs.

As I recovered from my breakdown, I started to ask myself, *What if I just said no?*

Really.

I started to wonder what would happen if I changed the choices on the table. No longer would I have to choose between what people wanted from me and what I wanted for myself. Instead, my choices were to continue living "one more thing" away from a total break down or freedom.

That choice was easy. I definitely didn't want to continue living on the edge of my mental and emotional limits, and I most certainly wanted to feel free. So that became the litmus test. I started making decisions based on where the outcomes would land me – whether they'd make me feel more overwhelmed or bring me joy and satisfaction. When I put it that way, the decision to choose me became much easier.

And asking for help did, too.

I realized that it's unfair of me to expect that I can do everything for everyone all the time – and still have enough left over for myself. In fact, I discovered that I had it all wrong. I deserve more than the leftovers.

Choosing only what I have the capacity for – and asking for help with the things I don't – made space for me to take care of my first responsibility – me. I also had to admit that everyone alive wasn't incompetent or untrustworthy. I had simply allowed myself to rely on the wrong people for the wrong roles. When it came to asking for help, I realized that I had to be clear that I was asking the right person for the right help, and I also had to be clear that they wanted to – and could – provide the assistance needed.

In other words, rather than being hyper-independent, I learned to be more discerning. And with that discernment came a greater ability to be vulnerable. It definitely took strength to carry all I have, but it has taken greater strength and a deeper sense of self-awareness to say, "I've had enough. I don't have to do it all, and I'm not going to any longer."

And mean it.

SECRET 6

I'm Lonely

I'm an introvert.
I just enjoy my own company.
I can come and go as I please.
Maybe I don't need new friends.
I love living alone.
I just don't trust people like that.
I'm not on the hunt for a husband.
I'm good.

There's nothing inherently wrong with these statements. In fact, with the right motivation behind them, they're quite healthy. Personally, though, I've used them as excuses for why I've avoided close relationships, both romantic and platonic.

I've shared with you how my heart has been broken and how I'd turned what were once healthy boundaries into impenetrable barriers. While I thought I was protecting myself from being hurt again by people I love, I actually ended up secluding myself emotionally from the world.

The thing about loneliness is that it doesn't always look the way people expect it to. It doesn't necessarily mean sitting alone, silently, in a dark room. It can be subtle, masked by busyness and over-productivity. Lonely people can be in a crowd and still feel incredibly alone. They can have lives full of activity and still ache for real connection. For me, loneliness wasn't just a lack of companionship – it was an emptiness that came from being emotionally isolated.

After my second divorce, I learned to dissociate my emotions from my interpersonal dealings. I became a people-user. I discovered that when I turned my emotions off, I could get what I wanted from people – or only have the level of interaction with them that I desired – without the risk of getting hurt. I was proud of the fact that I could have a private relationship with someone, and in public, treat them like a complete stranger.

My modus operandi was to be in a position where I could bail on them if things got more serious than I was willing to be or where I could hurt them before they hurt me.

It was a twisted way of taking care of my heart, but it was the best I could do. I'd given myself to others and they'd hurt me with seemingly no regrets. I had been loyal to them, but when it was their turn to reciprocate, their loyalty was nowhere to be found. I had dealt with them with grace and understanding, but when it was my turn to be forgiven there was no forgiveness available to me.

And so, my response was to turn off my desire for love and affection. I told myself that my family was all I needed, and that friends and lovers were unnecessary. If I wanted anything more, I could simply engage just enough to soothe whatever need I had and move on.

At the time, I had no regrets. I became selfish and destructive. I stopped caring about how my actions affected other people. It didn't matter if I destroyed marriages, relationships, or friendships – I didn't care. I stopped waiting to be a recipient. I turned into a taker. I was finally giving myself what I believed I was owed.

While this was a short period in my life – about a year – it was a tempestuous one. I was acting completely against my nature, and I was torn. I'm a giver and a lover – and treating people like a commodity went against everything inside me. The entire time I was acting out, my heart was screaming for more, because deep down I wanted something totally different: safety, security, warmth, love.

I wanted to reach out and form friendships and be part of "girlfriend circles". I wanted best friends and to go on girls' trips. I desired to date and to develop a loving, healthy relationship with a man. I didn't want to pretend to be friendly; I really wanted to be.

But it terrified me to be open. The risk seemed too great. Allowing people to have access to the "softest" parts of me made me susceptible to more hurt, more abandonment, and more rejection. I just couldn't stomach it.

I started avoiding networking events, social gatherings, and any place where I'd have to engage in small talk or meet new people. I filled my calendar with work, travel, and errands, convincing myself that I was just too busy for personal relationships. I would sit at home on Friday nights, scrolling through social media, seeing people living the life I secretly longed for, and telling myself that I didn't want what they had.

I thought I was content. But I was jealous. I envied the laughter, the camaraderie, the joy that others seemed to experience effortlessly. I would see groups of women out for brunch, taking trips, or simply enjoying each other's company and feel a pang of longing so deep it was almost physical. But I buried that feeling because I was too afraid to admit that I wanted it too. I couldn't bring myself to confront the reality that I wanted more than I was allowing myself to have.

Faking It

I pretended I was ok with being emotionally walled off from people. I was fine with sharing pieces of me, but I made sure no one had full access. Even with family and the few people whom I dared to label as friends, I never managed to be fully open. I hadn't just privatized my heart; I had shut down its ability to connect altogether.

Eventually, though, I grew tired of feeling alone.

I looked around and realized that what I was doing wasn't working, and it didn't feel good. It wasn't enough. I craved more. I wanted to feel like I belonged. But I'd successfully frozen everyone out, and now I was the one left standing in the cold.

I know I was reaping what I had sown. I'd recklessly burned bridges, I'd secluded myself, and I'd sabotaged nearly every effort anyone made to get close to me. I was left standing on the sidelines, watching others enjoy their friendships, relationships, and marriages, and all I could do was wish I had what they had.

And then my daughter left for college – and I really was alone. The only thing that made me feel better was to double down on the pretense. I told myself that work, shopping, and travel were all I needed. I could live in "rich single auntie" mode forever and be content.

But my heart secretly yearned for more, and the more I pretended I didn't need meaningful connections outside of family, the more my heart cried out for them. The distance between the life I was living and the life I wanted continued to grow, but I didn't know how to make the reconnection. I'd become so good at keeping people at a distance (or away altogether), I didn't know how to allow them in.

I tried rekindling old friendships and deepening existing ones, but it felt odd. I couldn't seem to get past the hump of feeling like an outsider or an intruder. And when my attempts didn't work as planned, they became the proof I waved overhead as the reason why I kept to myself. They validated my self-sabotage and "proved" why I should never have reached out in the first place.

The risk of putting myself "out there" and being rejected wasn't one I was willing to take. What if I opened up and reached out, and they turned me away? The fear was paralyzing, and eventually I just decided that I was better off alone than risking rejection again. So, anytime someone would express an interest in me or invite me out to socialize, I'd find excuses not to attend, or I'd cancel and retreat into my own little world. Every time, I felt a mix of relief and regret. Relief because I didn't have to pretend, and regret because I still felt alone.

But there I was – a single empty-nester, and I didn't like the idea of going through the rest of my life without partnership or companionship. I wondered whether I'd ever find another intimate relationship. *Would I really have to go through life without my "person"?*

I Did This

The worst part of my "big breakdown" was how alone I felt. Leading up to it, people would ask what was going on or how I was doing, and I'd hide the truth. I'd tell them I was just having a bad day or physically feeling unwell, but I never shared what was really happening inside.

I was so afraid of what the people around me would think or what they'd do if they found out that I was living in constant fear of death, or if they knew I was still devastated about losing people I really cared about. I kept the full breadth and depth of it all hidden. The problems they thought I was having weren't the actual problems I was having.

I'm sure I frustrated them as much as I frustrated myself. It's extremely difficult to be supportive of someone when you don't know the true nature of their need. All you can really offer is "It's going to work out, I'm sure," or "Everything will be ok." And while those statements are encouraging and helpful in many situations, when someone is on "the brink", they tend to fall flat. They only signal to the recipient that the situation appears hopeless.

When I called out for help that night, no one answered. I was hoping that God would supernaturally inspire someone to ring my doorbell to check on me in the nick of time, but He didn't. I thought maybe someone would "just happen" to call and I could tell them that I wasn't ok – but the phone never rang.

It was the loudest silence I'd ever heard. And in that moment, it hit me: all the things I'd done had worked. I wasn't alone because I lacked people who loved me; I was alone because I'd become an expert at keeping them all at bay. I'd done this to myself.

It took being faced with death to realize just how much I'd closed myself off to the world, and I didn't know how to open myself back up. Even with a therapist, "putting myself back out there" was extremely difficult, because my mind knew what I should do, but my heart wouldn't give me permission to do it.

The Gift That Keeps on Giving

Now, let me pause to clarify: I am not saying that all single women are inherently unhappy and lonely, or that we must have a gaggle of friends to feel like we're living full, meaningful lives. Being single and having a small, loving circle is amazing; I want to be clear about that.

I'm talking to those of us who keep everyone away, including the people who have demonstrated that they love us and that they want to love us. I'm addressing those of us who avoid relationships out of fear, and who believe that pain is the only thing that can ever come with vulnerability. We are the ones carrying this heavy secret.

We believe we must shoulder everything that happens in our lives alone, and not just because we're self-reliant. Our truth is that we were hurt, and our salve for that pain has been to shut everyone out and fill our lives with so many tasks and "things" that we'd forget how we really feel. And to make sure we never feel that pain again.

What we really want is to feel seen. And that can only happen when we let people in. When we allow ourselves to be vulnerable and open, we give them the opportunity to see us for who we really are. And when we are seen, we are known, and we can be loved not for the masks we wear, but for the people we truly are.

Being seen is powerful. It's validating, affirming, and deeply comforting. It reminds us that we are not alone in this world, that we are connected to others in meaningful ways, and that we are worthy of love and belonging. It doesn't matter how independent, successful, or affluent you are. We all want relationships that hold space for us to be vulnerable, open, and trusting. And while the term "safe space" is often overly used, it's perfect here. We need safe spaces and safe people – the kind that allow us to dismantle our walls and experience the flow of love and trust we desire.

For me, breaking the cycle of loneliness was a deliberate choice. It was an intentional decision to prioritize connection over fear. The journey is not always easy, and there have certainly been moments when retreating seemed like a better option than forging ahead – when I'd rather pull back into my safe, solitary space. But I had to remember that real growth, real healing, and real joy come from stepping outside of my comfort zone.

Choosing connection meant choosing to believe that love and friendship are worth the risk. I had to let go of my need for control and embrace the uncertainty that comes with human relationships. I had to take the chance that I could be hurt, but I also had to trust that the benefits of love, connection, and belonging could far outweigh my fear of rejection.

If there's one thing I've learned, it's that I'm not the only one who has hidden her loneliness behind her smile, her busy schedule, and statements like, "I'm good." Deep down, there are many of us who are yearning for more. We want to be loved. We want to be seen. We want to belong.

We are not meant to walk this life alone. There are powerful relationships destined for us. We're meant to share our lives with others. The desire for that isn't something to be ashamed of; it's something to embrace.

I chose to break free from the walls I'd built, so I could step into the fullness of life and love that was waiting for me.

I'm Lonely

It was scary, for sure, but it's been totally worth it.

SECRET 7

I Don't Belong Here

A male friend and I were having a conversation about relationship needs once, and I shared that reassurance is important to me. I told him I like to be affirmed and told I'm loved. I want to know that everything between us is ok, and the person wants to be with me. He was so surprised by my response! When I asked why, he revealed that it was because I seemed to already be complete – that I appear to be confident and have everything I need. To him, I gave the impression that my life was full and well organized, and there was nothing about which I'd need to be reassured.

I can't say this is the first time I've ever heard this. Because I am the proverbial "independent woman", people have assumed that I have it all together. In fact, I have been told more than once that people tend to avoid me for one of two reasons: they either feel they must be at a certain level to approach me, or they perceive that I have everything I need, with no room for anyone else. Apparently, I come across as "full," and to them, trying to fit into my life would be pointless because there's no place for them.

Now, I recognize that I've created an image that leads people to these assumptions. On social media, it's been easy to highlight the parts of my life that make me look like a superstar and sugar-coat – or hide altogether – the moments when I've felt like a nobody. And before you judge me, understand that it's something most social media users do. It makes us all feel better to carefully curate our online personas, where we smile for pictures that make people think we live lavish, happy lives they should envy, so people won't notice the excruciating emotional pain we're in.

In fact, if you use social media, you're probably more likely to post content that makes you appear to be living your best life, when you're at your lowest emotionally. There's something about those little blue thumbs and red hearts that take us out of our reality and allow us to live vicariously through the smiling person in the pictures we post. They provide an emotional escape from what we're actually feeling.

At one point, I found myself doing that a lot – using social media to escape my real life and to project my successes in ways that made people think that all I did was "win win win, no matter what" – when I was taking "loss, loss, loss after loss". I was hiding that part of my life, because I didn't believe people could handle seeing that side of me – the losing side. Oh, for sure, there were people who said that showing the "not fun" times was a way to display authenticity and connect with people online more deeply, but I couldn't bring myself to do it. I could be serious and share about painful topics, but once I felt the sting of tears or the inkling of a lump in my throat, I'd immediately shut down.

The Wonderful Wizard of Oz

I believe everyone wants to belong. Maybe not to large groups, fraternities, or sororities, but I think everyone needs a sense that they fit somewhere. Even if you're not a people person, your heart and mind desire places where they feel at ease, surrounded by similarities – likes, desires, hopes, goals.

I have often said that our individual purposes are like puzzle pieces – unique in their design and perfectly suited for the place they're supposed to fit. It's what makes each of us different, yet complementary to others. It's how we know we're where we're supposed to be. Having a sense that you belong makes you feel comfortable, and it reinforces your sense of identity.

There are quite a lot of people who say they don't care whether they fit in; they're happy all by themselves. But there are some of us who want and need to be connected with others and to feel like we are a valuable part of a group or community. The challenge for many of us – well for me – is that after collecting all these secrets and carrying around the pain I've endured over my lifetime, I desired to be connected to others, but found it hard to feel safe enough to authentically connect.

Years of pretending to be older, smarter, and more successful than I was didn't just leave me in constant competition with myself, it left me feeling afraid to allow people to see the real me – the one who was working hard to actually *be* those things. I was always afraid that if they found out that I wasn't the image I projected, they'd call me a fraud or a fake. They'd discover that the person who looked like she had it all together was putting on a show.

Remember in the Wizard of Oz, how Dorothy and her crew were so scared and intimidated by Mr. Great and Powerful? All it took for his whole rouse to fall apart was a curious little puppy, who pulled back that green velvet curtain to show us that he was just some guy with a machine that made him appear more formidable than he was. The Wizard *was* a fraud, though. He had all those people thinking he was something he wasn't.

For a long time, that's how I perceived myself – as someone who was insignificant, but who – via smoke and mirrors – had manufactured a persona that people thought was powerful and influential. I felt like I was the one behind that curtain, orchestrating a show – ringing the bells and blowing the whistles to keep people from seeing the girl behind it all.

I wasn't a fraud, but I couldn't see that. In fact, I was surprised any time someone was impressed with my resume, or when they "oohed and ahhed" during the reading of my professional bio. It wasn't that I didn't truly deserve the admiration. It was like I'd forgotten the work I'd put into earning those accolades and achieving those goals. I'd hear their words, but it would feel like they were talking about someone else.

Life and pain had taught me that those words are often empty – that people can look right at you, praise you, and call you amazing – and still reject you. I had discovered that people can smile at you, and even act like they want to be friends with you, but that doesn't mean they accept, respect, or value you.

My response to that, both personally and professionally, was to hide the parts of myself that I thought people didn't like. Every time I showed a part of myself to someone, and they rejected it, I hid it away, so that "next time", it wouldn't be a reason I wasn't accepted. It was extremely painful to allow someone into the inner sanctum of my life, only for them to recoil once there, as if what I'd revealed was too much for their mind to handle. Or that what they saw when they got behind the curtain was too gruesome to withstand.

It's one thing to think I'm a cool person to know from a distance. It's a "whole 'nother" thing to discover that the person on social media, in the bun and colorful glasses, is an entirely different woman when her hair is down and her bra is off. The person they thought they knew turned out to be a carefully curated persona, and they're now faced with someone who is a stranger to them. And once the reality sank in that befriending an introverted entrepreneur who regularly battles anxiety and depression isn't easy, their desire for friendship would often shift drastically.

So, when others decided that the "real" me was too much, and they exited my life, it would reinforce the idea that no one wanted or could handle the real Rhonda, so I could never show up as her. I tucked those parts of myself away so they wouldn't be an issue in the future, but it never seemed to work. All it did was make me paranoid that I'd lose everyone who got close to me.

An Ugly Bouquet

The words I'd heard from others over the years became a mantra I started repeating to myself: "You're too much". I had internalized their inability to see my value and began questioning it myself. I'd find myself silent and shying away from the spotlight in influential spaces. I'd look around the room and mentally size myself up against the people there. And in my mind, I didn't measure up. I wasn't as rich as they were, as well connected, or as charismatic. I just didn't believe I belonged, and I questioned my ability to add value in those spaces.

By then, those seeds of rejection had blossomed into full-blown imposter syndrome. Despite all my accomplishments, degrees, and accolades, I always felt like the unqualified kid in the room. I rarely spoke up, and I almost never engaged. There's a saying that "it's better to be thought a fool than to open your mouth and remove all doubt". Well, that was a statement I lived by. The public had less of a chance of discovering that I was an intruder who didn't belong if I never opened my mouth and proved it.

But I Worked Hard for This

I had put a lot of effort into being the woman I thought people would want and accept. I made sure that she looked like them and talked like them, because *she* was my ticket in. She was the one who could be seen and respected in the spaces I wanted to belong.

Another reason I experienced the breakdown was because I didn't want the leaders and powerbrokers I was connected with to see me as a quitter. If I'd let go of the things that were not only making me physically and emotionally ill, but actually driving me insane, I'd only be giving these people the opportunity to think that I'd let go because I couldn't handle the task.

The crazy thing about it all is that it wouldn't have mattered whether I succeeded or failed. In that state of mind, I still wouldn't have felt accepted because it really wasn't their rejection that had me abusing myself the way I was. It was my rejection of me that was the culprit.

Instead of leaning into my authentic self and requiring her to be honored and loved – by me and everyone else – I rejected her. I hid her. I violated myself the same way others had. It took a while for me to realize what I'd been doing, but once that light bulb came on, I thought, *How could anyone value a person I don't even value?* I had been teaching the world how to treat the real Rhonda. I'd been showing them that when you see her, you put her away, you reject her. She's not valuable enough to be seen.

What a revelation that was! Once I discovered that all the good parts of myself were hidden in the basement, far out of sight – I started to understand just how toxic imposter syndrome had been to me. All this time, I'd been thinking that others didn't value me and that I didn't belong, and I was wrong. I was the one who had buried my most valuable assets and hid them from the public.

Takes One to Know One

What I mistook for a lack of value or an inability to be loved for who I truly am was actually a misunderstanding of my own identity – and failing to see that I wasn't designed to "fit in" everywhere. What I didn't know at the time was there's a room for everybody. Just like the "old folks" used to say, "There's a lid for every pot". It's not a statement that's only reserved for moments when you've encountered two ugly people kissing. It means that real will recognize real – that when you find your people, you know it, and they do too.

The people in the rooms where I belonged helped me change what I thought about myself because they fanned the flames of what I'd recently unearthed – that I didn't have to accept everyone's evaluation of me, nor did I have to allow rejection to be the one to decide whether or not I had value. They made me feel safe enough to share myself authentically – slowly, of course – but when I did, there was no rejection, only love, respect, and acceptance. No longer did I have to believe the lie that people would always see the real me as "too much". The places where I found belonging made space for all the facets of me, including the ones behind the curtain.

For many of us, it's a kneejerk reaction to hide the parts of ourselves others have made us believe were ugly. But truthfully, these are the very things that make us beautiful and special. Unfortunately, someone who lacked the ability to truly see us got the opportunity to influence us in ways they never should have. And so, their words became an additional lock on the muzzle that silenced us. It was another trick to get us to spend our lives shrinking back instead of standing tall. All it took was for the belief that we are not valuable to take root. Once it did, it gained the power to undermine everything in our lives.

It could be said that we merely need to affirm more positive things to ourselves to be reminded that we're not imposters. And while that may be partly true, I believe there's more to it. We feel inadequate because we're trying to contort ourselves into something that's appealing to everyone, and that's simply not possible. Even with the world's most respected artworks, no two people value or enjoy them the same way. Yet not one painting, sketch, or sculpture changes its beauty to appeal to the beholder.

The real issue lies in the extent to which we're able to see that we're not broken, or ugly, or too much. It's up to us to create the truth about ourselves.

What If, What If, What If

Imposter syndrome has been an ever-present voice in my life that whispered, "You're not good enough yet." It spoke lies that were rooted in my fear. Fear of being seen as less than. Fear of being judged. Fear that if I showed one flaw, I'd be exposed as a fraud who didn't qualify for success, love, or respect.

I struggled with this debilitating mindset not because I'm incapable, but because I'd convinced myself that I had to be damn-near perfect to be enough. And I knew I could never hit that mark. So, every time I started a new project or took on a new role, fear would kick in. What if they realize

I'm not as good as they think I am? What if I mess up? What if I'm not really meant to be here?

Imposter syndrome caused me to talk myself out of more opportunities than I care to admit – all because I felt unworthy. Every "what if" was a noose that choked my creativity and confidence, leaving me to believe that someone more "qualified" or "together" should take the lead.

Any time I actually did step forward, I felt triggered by every critique and every comment that wasn't glowing feedback, because deep down, I had already been doubting myself. Eventually, I realized that "they" weren't the problem; their words were. They'd teamed up with my own inner critic, confirming and reinforcing my insecurities and my rejection issues.

Come Out, Come Out Wherever You Are

My struggle with imposter syndrome wasn't as simple as having "low self-esteem", nor was it merely a failure to see that I had value. It was my belief that others couldn't see my value that made me put myself through that self-inflicted abuse. And so, changing that belief had to start in the same place the buck stopped – with me.

As long as we conceal who we truly are, we'll always feel like the world won't accept us. And we'll be right. People can't value what they cannot see.

The only way we can show them is to come out of hiding.

Part 2

How Did We Get Here?

CHAPTER 8

Where In the WORLD Did This Come From?

Yo' mama.

Well...

Maybe not *your* mother. More than likely, it came from your mother's great-great grandmother's mother. A matriarch who holds a distant place in your bloodline commonly referred to as "the ancestors". For her, strength wasn't a cliché. It was a necessity. Strength was the only thing that helped her survive in a time when she and everyone who looked like her were considered no more than property, used and abused at the hands of an enslaver. There was no other way to live through constant trauma other than to learn how to remove yourself from the mental and physical anguish that was so much a part of your daily experience.

Being strong kept you alive. It kept you from succumbing to the grief of being snatched from the only home you've ever known and watching every single person you love – including your children – treated like worthless objects. It kept you from ending your own life, when you felt like you had no hope, knowing that there was no end in sight – that there was no one coming to save you and your loved ones.

Strength allowed you to find dignity in the most humiliating of circumstances. It allowed you to find "silver linings" wherever you could, and it helped you to hope that perhaps one day, you or someone you loved would find freedom. Strength wasn't something to be proud of or to commend someone for being. It was just the requirement for survival.

I think of the many Black women I have had the honor of getting to know through research, and one in particular comes to mind often. Her name was Biddie Mason. She was born enslaved, and as an adult was made to walk behind her enslavers' carriage from Georgia to Utah, nursing her first baby. While she was there, she not only discovered how to deliver and care for babies, but she was also put in charge of other enslaved women. By the time her caravan moved to California, with her and those she supervised (including children), walking once again, she was an expert midwife.

Even though she couldn't read or write, Biddie managed to win her freedom in court, and she made sure that the women with her were freed as well. By the time her life was over, she'd reached the status of being California's most sought-after midwife, and it didn't matter to anyone what color she was. During her lifetime, she started First A.M.E Church, ran a prison ministry and a traveler's aid center, and amassed a net worth of well over $3 million.

The point of that little history lesson – and please, go read about her if you've never heard of her – is that quite often when we read stories like hers, we are awestruck, and we think, *What she did was incredible!* And, while that's not wrong, the truth of the matter is she spent most of her life withstanding trauma. Still, she was able to care for herself, everyone around her, build a career, and amass significant wealth.

Sound familiar?

Certainly, I don't mean to insinuate that our present-day struggles compare in any way, shape, or form to Biddie's. What I am saying, however, is that she took what worked for her and taught it to her daughters and the women around her. She not only told them that they needed to be strong; she modeled it for them, and they followed suit.

She showed her daughters how to withhold tears and emotions when confronted by their enslavers, because she knew that would only fuel their fire. "Holding it together" was a means of personal protest, a way to hold on to some shreds of dignity and self-worth. Her daughters learned to take whatever came their way, to suppress their emotions, and to keep moving forward.

Not only that, she also taught them how to protect themselves and their families, and to be the glue that holds the family together. She showed them that – with tenacity – it is possible to thrive, even in the harshest of environments. Matriarchs served as young women's examples of how to make something good, even when you have next to nothing.

Our foremothers did what was necessary to survive, often pressing forward despite unimaginable pain. They lived with their fears – and the possibility of death – on a daily basis. For them, weakness wasn't an option if they wanted to live. And for the generations of Black women that came after them, the ability to survive and achieve was founded upon this mindset.

In our lifetimes, we probably witnessed the strength of our own mothers and grandmothers. We watched them hold our families together without jobs outside the home, sometimes knowing that there was a family across town with whom they shared their husbands.

Still, we observed the way those matriarchs conducted themselves. They shouldered whatever pain or humiliation they may have felt and continued to make stable homes for their husbands and children. They did all the emotional and mental heavy lifting for the family, and they made sure everyone else's needs were met, even if theirs were not.

These women had no choice but to endure. Their options were limited; they were operating within a system that didn't even acknowledge their existence. We all know that it wasn't until 1970s that women could even have bank accounts in their name. So, of course, these women had no choice but to stay in unhealthy marriages and make the best of what was – for some of them – an extremely toxic home life. Many of us never saw these women – truly strong Black women – lash out at their spouses for the situations they had to live in. They, like their mothers, had been taught that there was no place for their pain, so it was best to put it away and ignore it.

Then in the 1990s, the traditional "Black family" took a hit. Thanks to the war on drugs and increasingly oppressive systemic racism, Black women became the core of the family unit. It was then that the "strong Black woman" trope became a badge of honor. It was glamorized on TV and in movies, and it was always the same: the stressed out, overworked, 30-something, single woman, who was struggling to raise good kids and make ends meet. Somehow, though, she defied the odds, building a better life for her kids, all while winning employee of the month and earning straight A's in night school. To be a "Strong Black Woman" during that time meant knowing how to do a lot with very little, achieving excellence with the bare minimum, and "making it" against all odds. It signified that you were a fighter, a survivor—a winner.

But now, here we are in 2025, and sis is tired.

Tired of having to think for everyone else.

Tired of carrying the household on our backs with no one to share the load.

Tired of being so busy we never have time for ourselves.

Tired of showing up for people who won't show up for us.

Tired of pretending we're okay when we're not.

We are tired.

And we are done.

Many of us have hit a wall of realization. That after all these years of looking out for everyone else, there really isn't anyone looking out for us. We made the mistake of thinking that if we played by the rules, society would treat us fairly. Somehow, we allowed ourselves to believe that with all the accolades and accomplishments, with years of expertise and track-records of success, society would finally say, "You're worthy."

But when it was time for that to happen, when one of us finally had the opportunity to attain the most powerful role in the world, we found ourselves back in that old cycle of being passed over in favor of someone who's the very opposite of appropriate for the role. The 2024 presidential election was a perfect example of this.

Though we weren't all running for president, many of us took the loss personally. It wasn't the loss of the election that hurt as much as feeling like we'd been played. And it was a gut punch. We couldn't get out of bed. Some of us couldn't function or rest, and we couldn't quite figure out why we felt the way we did. It wasn't just anger; nor was it merely frustration.

We were triggered.

We were emotionally snatched back to the times when we shared an idea that didn't receive much enthusiasm until some mediocre white guy restated it, and they treated him like he'd just invented teleporting – like it wasn't US who'd said it first. It reminded us of the times when people smiled in our faces but acted against us in private. We found that there were people who publicly said they cared about our lives and our wellbeing, but then anonymously chose their own interests and our detriment. It snapped us back to the moments when we should have been chosen and weren't. We weren't feeling this way because a more qualified candidate won, but because society clearly demonstrated that it would rather have *anybody* other than a Black woman.

No, Thanks. Y'all Got It

That's when we had to accept that "working twice as hard to be seen as half as good" isn't even the glass ceiling anymore. A harsh reality hit home: it doesn't matter how hard you work, or how consistently you come through for others, it's not enough. It's never enough. No matter how high you go. It will never be enough.

It was eye opening, and it made us face the truth – if we don't have our backs, nobody else will.

That revelation did it. It pushed us to finally take off the capes, remove the masks, and set down everything that didn't contribute to our healing, our happiness, our growth, and our peace. A movement broke out – one which made it clear that we were finished being the champion for everyone's causes, with no one to don a cape for ours. We finally saw what remains when you live in a deficit and pour from empty vessels: when everyone takes their ball and goes home, we are the ones left with nothing for ourselves.

For so long, we've lived suppressing bitterness, overwhelm, and resentment in our lives. It's part of our daily routine to step out of who we are and into who we need to be to survive each day. For us, code-switching is more than merely changing our language; it's the way we temporarily become different people altogether.

Even when we're back at home, we don't give ourselves a break, do we? We just swap one mask one for another. As we deal with the challenges that come with raising a family, nurturing a marriage, negotiating family relationships, and maintaining a household, we often find ourselves putting considerable effort into making those things work. So when we're not overachieving in the workplace, we're overachieving at home in the roles of "great mom", "amazing wife", and "meticulous homemaker".

We put so much emphasis on the wellbeing of everyone else, we forget that at the center of it all, we are part of the equation, too. Our needs for rest and renewal are real, yet they often go unmet. Of course, we could blame the people around us for not returning to us the energy they receive from us – but the truth is we've taught them that neglecting us is ok. So, our emptiness isn't all their fault. We give them the time we could be taking to restore our own minds, bodies, and souls, believing that being a good partner, parent, friend, or employee means being bad to yourself.

No, Seriously. We're Done.

Well now, we're through being strong for everyone else and not having strength when we need it. In fact, many of us don't want to be strong at all anymore. We've found that our way of being strong simply enables the rest of the world to receive more of us than their fair share – because that's what we've been giving. We've been self-sacrificing for far too long.

The big question that's being asked is – What do we do now? How do we pick up the pieces of ourselves and put them back together? They say what doesn't kill you makes you stronger, but I want to know: stronger for what exactly? Because let's be real. The "stronger" train we were on was definitely killing us – if not physically, then certainly emotionally and mentally.

In the days following my breakdown, when all I could do was look out the window or scroll through Hulu, I had zero strength. I didn't want to help anyone. I wasn't concerned about their problems. I didn't have any answers. All I had was my shattered life, and as much as I wanted to jump back in the saddle and get back to the hustle and grind, neither my body nor my mind would allow me to.

And so, rest became my primary focus. I didn't have much of a choice, really. I couldn't function. My only option was to relax and receive what God was trying to give me – peace. It was time to give myself permission to do absolutely nothing, and to be responsible for as much.

During that time, I also did a lot of thinking about how I'd allowed myself to get to such a low place, and I concluded that I held an extremely toxic sense of strength. My idea of being strong wasn't just surviving all life had thrown at me; it was also surviving my criticisms and my self-abuse for not being better, for not doing more. I was carrying the oppressive weight of my responsibilities and insecurities and trying to outrun my fears — all at the same time.

Imagine, If You Will...

I don't know if you can picture it in your mind's eye, but just imagine a woman, draped in her accomplishments, with everything she loves and feels responsible for on her shoulders. On her back is a heavy sack filled with her secret traumas and fears. She's enclosed in bars — like a mobile jail cell — and in there with her are the whispering voices of her insecurities and her misinformed self-critic. They surround her, taunting her.

Her arms are outstretched; she's reaching outside the cell — not to be rescued, but to reach rows and rows of plates spinning on very thin sticks. She's running between them all, dragging herself, the load she's carrying, and the cell she's in. She appears to have a pained expression on her face, like she's expending great effort to do what she's doing. But if you look closely, you can see the tears streaming down her face.

What she wants more than anything is the peace she can see just beyond those rows of plates, but it remains outside of her reach. She can't seem to keep all the plates spinning on her own long enough to get to it. But she can't stop and allow herself to grasp what she truly wants, because the voices in the cell have made her believe that if just one plate hits the floor, the world will know the truth. They'll see those tears, and they'll realize she couldn't handle it all. She never could. She wasn't strong enough.

Now, it probably goes without saying that the woman I described was me.

But... is it you, too?

I mean, if you were to be really honest about what it feels like to be you, right now, would you say that it feels a lot like someone who is doing everything in her power to meet everyone else's expectations and needs, take care of all the things going on in her life, while ignoring — or actively running from — the person who needs her attention the most? If this imagery resonates with you, it's because you've been trying to "just get past" one thing after the other, but the list of things never ends. You think you need a massage, a girls' trip, or a couple days off – when what you really need is to let it all go.

Let every single one of those plates crash to the ground.

Remove the responsibilities and obligations from your shoulders.

Release yourself from those secrets.

Silence all the voices.

And then, open the door and walk away from it all.

CHAPTER 9

Strength, Differently

Let's be honest. We're all ready to walk away because the strength we're using right now isn't benefiting us. It's not even helping us survive, because we're drowning. Perhaps more slowly than we would if we weren't flailing like crazy to stay afloat, but we're definitely going under.

And to add insult to injury, we can't (or won't) yell out for help because the secrets we've been carrying have strangled the voices out of us. We're so accustomed to managing this façade that speaking up for help feels like telling the world we're failures. There's literally nothing about this version of "strength" that pays off the way we think it will. It simply leads to more shame, more guilt, and more hiding.

Make no mistake: the decision to let it all go is a scary one. I'll be honest with you about that. But trust me: you'd much rather make the decision for yourself than have your body and mind make it for you. They don't play fair. When they've had enough, they flip all the light switches off, and they go sit down.

So, we've got to be clear about what it means to "let go", otherwise, we won't be able to do it. It's not some nebulous idea that a Disney princess sung about, either. It's giving yourself permission to let the sh*t hit the fan. I know, it's something you'd normally never do. Because you don't let anything get by you – you don't miss deadlines, calls, or texts. You don't drop the ball – you have the answers when the world has questions. You're never out of place – you cover your backside, and everyone else's too. You are the one the world counts on, because they can. You always come through.

I get it.

But, I also get that you're exhausted. I understand that not only do you want to release yourself from all you've been carrying so you can rest, you also don't want to pick any of it back up once your respite is over. You want peace – and not a temporary peace, either. You want a lasting sense of peace that allows you to continue to be the amazing woman you are, but in a way that feeds your soul rather than sucking the life out of it. You want to be free of everyone's expectations and limitations. You want to get off the performative hamster wheel and be who you truly are.

You want to reclaim your voice and your power.

Well, there's only one way for you to do that. You've got to redefine what strength looks like, because it's certainly not dragging that cell around, running to keep all those plates spinning in the air.

This is the point where you acknowledge that hiding the pain of your trauma has not only been ineffective in minimizing its impact in your everyday life. The secrets you're carrying are also slowing you down and keeping you from living the way you desire to live. I often say that we don't survive all we go through just for the PTSD and therapy bills, and it's true – that wasn't the point of the experience.

You went through all that so you could learn from it, heal, and release it. Healing is an important part of the process because when we allow ourselves to truly recover from the painful things that happen to us, our wholeness makes us stronger and smarter so we're better equipped to face the next challenge. We don't win over trauma just so that we can drag it around with us forever.

Redefining strength means learning how to show up differently – for yourself and for others. It's learning how to "eat the meat and spit out the bones". In other words, the healthy version of strength allows you to hold on to what's healthy for you and reject what's not. It's a total mind shift that moves you from feeling voiceless to operating boldly in your power.

The only prerequisite for redefining strength in your life is the decision to release what it has meant for you thus far. You must be willing to get off the path of self-sacrificing and making yourself small for others, and you must be open to adopting new behaviors that allow you to show up fully and authentically as your whole, healed self.

Ok, So Maybe Kelly Clarkson Was Right

Once I realized that my idea of "being strong" was warped and needed to be discarded, I was able to admit that this distorted definition was at the root of my inability to deal with my pain, set it down, and leave it. I realized that I was carrying it all because I'd been taught that's what strong Black women are supposed to do.

I discovered that Kelly Clarkson was actually right when she sang, "What doesn't kill you makes you stronger". But she should have included a disclaimer. The things that we gain victory over don't make us strong so that we can carry the carcasses of our trauma across our back. Simply enduring trauma is not what makes you strong. You really gain strength when you are willing to go through the process of healing. That is where you discover what you're made of and gain new skills and strategies for withstanding the next season.

The things you've faced and survived should only live in your head as reminders that you're a conqueror, not that you're a carrier.

Every traumatic event and painful season equipped you to succeed in the days that would come and suited you with compassion for others who are where you once were. That was the purpose of the pain! Not to saddle you with secrets and weights to carry, but to prepare you for your future – to make sure that you were fully equipped to overcome whatever you'd be facing next and enable you to support to others who are walking in your footsteps from a place of overflow, rather than from a place of deficit.

Soft Is the New Strong

Our strength should be wielded like water – as a force that can soothe, sustain, or destroy. While gentle enough to caress the forehead of a newborn, water can also change the landscape of the Earth itself. The strength of water lies in its dual nature, as trickles that can smooth rocks and boulders, or as rapids strong enough to carve canyons through mountains.

This is what we're looking for. The freedom to release ourselves from the need to be strong all the time and to embrace our gentleness as much as we embrace our power. We desire to rest in our "softness" without judgment or ridicule. And when it's time for us to exert our power, we want to do so without being labeled angry or aggressive. We want to be free to only carry what we should – to release the painful seasons we were only meant to learn from, as well as those things that others should be carrying for themselves.

By discarding the toxic elements of strength, we give ourselves permission to reclaim what we've allowed the pain and trauma of our pasts to steal. We can finally release hyper-independence and embrace interdependence. We can set down our hard exteriors and embrace softness and ease. We can now lower our barriers and finally allow our hearts to receive.

Strength, when redefined, ceases to be a substitution for our identity, and becomes the tool for growth it was intended to be. So, we must reshape it to make it work for us, rather than against us. Admittedly, this doesn't happen without some discomfort, and in some instances, downright pain. This is unavoidable; it simply comes with the territory of transformation. It's the only way we can identify our secrets, recognize them as being harmful, forgive ourselves, let them go, and then adopt new, healthy ways of thinking and acting.

Like me, you may even discover that remnants of some of the secrets you thought you'd let go of, are still hanging on. You may have to admit that you still have feelings about some of the people and events you've pretended not to care about, and you'll have to admit that – despite your generous heart – you're tired of standing in the gap and being the tried-and-true safety net for the people in your life.

This is the part of the process where you get to embrace you. Where you acknowledge your feelings, identify where you're hurting, and actively put a plan in place that not only puts an end to your current pain, but which also helps you prevent future injury.

Beware, though. This process comes with some emotional risks. Your inner monologue – the misinformed voice that criticizes you and makes you feel insecure – will be chattier than ever, and it will make you question whether you've made the right choice. Only you know what your secrets truly are, and so you must do the work of uncovering them and shining a light on them.

You'll see transformation if you can commit to being honest with yourself about where you are and what you believe. Like faith, we all have a measure of strength, and the growth of your strength depends directly on what you feed it. Give it secrets, and your strength will grow them into cancers that will eat away at the length and quality of your life. Give it your authenticity and vulnerability, however, and your strength will free you and position you to be victorious over whatever lies ahead.

Go Ahead & Free Yourself

Your freedom lies in your willingness to tear down and rebuild - to discover the new things you'll do or say in lieu of the old things that used to keep you feeling trapped and stuck. Personally, I found a new way to live out loud – by changing how I think and what I say. I replaced my people-pleasing behaviors with actions that were in alignment with my capacity and my desires.

I also gave myself permission to consider and take care of myself first, guilt free. As they say in every pre-flight safety briefing, "Put your oxygen mask on first, before attempting to help others around you." I adopted this mantra wholeheartedly once I realized how much harm I was doing to myself in the name of helping others. Finally, I let the toxic selflessness go, and I acknowledged that I have needs and I am the one who's responsible for making sure they're met. This was the key to my transformation – adopting the belief that I am responsible for my own needs and making sure they are filled is not selfishness, it is healthy.

I also decided that I needed to flip the secrets I'd been holding onto into statements of power. I stopped allowing my trauma to make me believe that I'm not good enough, that I'm unworthy, or that I'll always be broken – and I started talking back. Once I realized the roots of these statements, I was able to dig them up, toss them out, and replace them with words that reminded me of the truth of who I am and who I'm created to be.

Reclaiming your voice and stepping into your power begins with this change. Before you can believe you deserve to live differently, you've got to adopt new ways of thinking. The messages you tell yourself on a daily basis will need to change. In times where you'd normally self-sacrifice or take on tasks that you neither have the desire nor the capacity for, you need to know what to say and why you're saying it. It's the only way to change your knee-jerk reaction.

These new-to-you truths are more than positive thinking or affirmations. They're the key to disarming the shame and guilt that will want to enter the conversation when you prioritize yourself over other people's thoughts about and expectations of you. You've got to know ahead of time that when you put up a boundary, you're protecting and honoring yourself. You're showing yourself some love!

It's time to show your secrets the door and usher in a mindset that will change how you allow yourself to be treated. Before you turn the page, though, make sure you're ready to leave your secrets behind – for good. Because you can't carry both. You can't continue to hide who you truly are and attempt to live as your most authentic self. You must be ready to embrace you – all of you – so that you can finally walk away from everything that's been holding you back and embrace the peace you've been pursuing for so long.

Part 3
The Truth

CHAPTER 10

My Secret: I Refuse to Be a Victim

The Truth: My Voice is My Superpower

The little girl who had her voice taken away grew up to be a woman who struggled to recover it. Even as an adult, at times it can still be difficult to speak up for myself without feeling guilt or shame. I still worry sometimes about what the fallout will be if and when I speak up for myself. But I learned that if one event could spark a lifetime of secret-keeping then one mindset shift can open the door to healing and freedom.

I had to get my voice back.

It started with the realization that I had kept this childhood secret, not to protect my abuser but to protect myself from becoming what I thought would be a stereotype or a statistic. I didn't want to be pitied – I still don't. But in my days of reflection and healing, I realized that it wasn't my abuser who had taken my voice – it was me. I had silenced the little girl who needed to speak the truth of what had happened to her. I had taken away her ability to heal by refusing to acknowledge – or perhaps understand – just how deeply she'd been hurt.

To heal, I'd need to get to the truth – I would need to acknowledge that deep down, I was not ok. I had to take a long honest look at all the times the secret had crippled me and view those moments for what they were – unresolved, misunderstood pain.

Getting my voice back started with that acknowledgement and understanding how it became a secret in the first place. I didn't feel a need to hide the abuse itself – but the label it had placed on me. I realized that I'd spend my entire life running from "victimhood" because I didn't to be seen that way.

What I now know is that my refusal to acknowledge that I had been victimized limited me. It's like healing a broken femur without having it properly set. You can still have a leg but it's never going to work at its optimal level. You learn to walk – maybe even run – with the limp, but it'll never function as well as it would have if it had been attended to and healed properly.

That was me – limping through life, as a powerful woman who still sometimes felt like that 3-year-old little girl who couldn't speak up and stand up for herself.

The Shift

The mindset shift that changed it all came with the realization that I am not what happened to me – what was done to me. The trauma and abuse I experienced was over. I had survived it. It wasn't until I could look at it and speak about it honestly that I became victorious over it. I was no longer just a survivor; I became a conqueror.

The moment I discovered that I didn't have to hide the fact that I was a victim of sexual abuse, the power of the silence was broken. I found myself talking about what happened to me from a place of wholeness and not from a place of injury. I retrieved the voice that I'd given away, and I learned that this part of me was just as powerful as the rest of me – the parts I'd allowed everyone to see. That's when the shift happened.

I also noticed something else. As much as I believe God has a plan for our lives, I believe the enemy of our souls, satan, has one too. He knows that fully empowered people are a threat to his kingdom. So, he starts early with his plan to cripple us – to stack the deck against us and in his favor – hoping that we will be so distant from God and resentful of Him that we'll abort our life's purpose and our God-given destiny. He wants us to be so confused and doubtful about who we are and the power we have that we pose no threat to him.

This keeps us on his side – where we are too afraid to be free of the trauma that not only follows us, but also from the pain we've been actively carrying around. He uses that early trauma against us so well that even when we are made free by God, we remain in the cage – door open – because we are more afraid of what might happen "out there" in the freedom we don't yet know, than in the bondage we're much more familiar with.

The shift happens the moment you decide to be free. That's when the door that's been holding your voice captive swings wide open. Just like you can walk into an office and speak with authority, you will start to do the same thing in other areas of your life. You really can walk out of the power of self-doubt, self-sabotage, and fear when you realize that whatever happened that took your voice was a trick to get you to shut up and forget you have real power.

The amazing thing is that the power is yours. It was assigned to you long before your earthly name was. It is your birthright, so you have the right to take it back. You don't have to continue living under the shadow of the trauma that was inflicted upon you, nor do you have to continue to fear that coming into the light will expose you in ways that will damage you further. Believe it or not, the very opposite will happen. When you shine the light on the pain that has kept you muzzled all these years, it instantly loses its power over you. In that moment you are free to not only think differently, but to live differently.

Your Strength Is in Your Voice

There's no magic formula or hoops to jump through to get your voice back. You don't have to click your heels together three times, and you don't have to conjure any spells. To reclaim your voice and your power, all you need is a willingness to be transparent and vulnerable.

If the biggest secret in your life had the power to silence you and cause you to live parts of your life in darkness, then releasing the secret has the power to let light into your life. First, though, you've got to come clean – you've got to be honest in ways you haven't before. You may feel led to share your story in a book. Or you may be called to share it in communities and in groups where other people can be helped and freed by your story.

Reclaiming your voice goes beyond just the acknowledgment of what happened to you; it's being willing to use that experience to unlock a door to someone else's freedom too. That's how you transform yourself from victim to victor. The very thing that was sent to steal your power and your voice is the same thing that when shared will bring healing for you and breakthrough for someone else.

Being transparent – sharing your story – fast tracks the healing process. Every time you give voice to your survivor, she grows as a victor. You take away the power from her abuser and return it to her. The stronger she becomes, the more she wants to share it with others who are where she once was. She becomes a key that releases imprisoned voices for generations to come.

Now, I'll admit that it's not always easy to jump right into transparency. It can be more complex than it sounds. Opening up about a secret you've held most of your life can be down-right scary.

That's where accountability comes in – or your support system. You need to first share your story with a therapist or another trusted person who can help you process what you have been through and who can help you find the words to articulate an event you may never have put words to before. It's hard to tell a story when you don't know the words!

This was the case for me. When the memory of the abuse I'd experienced resurfaced, I shared it first with my therapist. The hardest part wasn't discussing what had happened – it was finding the words to express how I felt about it and figuring out which words I wanted to use about what had happened and the impact it had on me. I had never verbalized any of what had taken place – ever. The only conversations I'd had about it occurred in my head.

So, when it came time to share what I'd remembered, the words seemed foreign, odd. It was strange talking about it out loud and it seemed even stranger that I was talking about me. But talking about it in therapy gave me the words to share with you. It was also where I realized my anger wasn't as much about what had happened to me as it was about the labels those actions placed on me. And it was in therapy is where I became aware that I was the one who continued to take away the voice of "little" Rhonda. I hadn't been protecting her – I'd been silencing her.

Had I not been open to talking about it with someone who knew how to walk with me through those memories and feelings, I may not have discovered my biggest secret of all.

So, sharing your story with someone (preferably a trained mental health professional) is a must. You'll be giving yourself a safe space to get accustomed to talking about what happened in a way that makes you feel empowered and not small. You'll develop a language that doesn't skirt the details but doesn't retraumatize you either. Allow yourself to go through the process of transforming your mind and your mindset. Give yourself the grace to take as many baby steps as you need to.

With the support of people who comprise your safe space, take advantage of opportunities to share your story at the level you feel comfortable. You'll be amazed at the number of people who will come out of the woodwork, whispering "me too". For many of us, that's where transparency begins – with those two simple words. And before you know it, you're finding a new freedom because you're no longer hiding, you're healing. All the while, others who are in the struggle you were once in now know there's hope. Because of you, they're able to see that what they're going through will pass, and they will be ok. All because you raised your voice – if for nothing else but to speak those two little words.

A Win-Win for Everybody

Once you have a taste of freedom and realize the healing power of your voice – of your story – you'll never keep quiet again. You'll be increasingly willing to share your experience to help anyone who needs it, and you'll discover that sharing your story isn't just an accelerator of your own healing, it's a cup filler too. Just as a pipe can't deliver water without itself getting wet, you can't share your own healing with others and not gain a little more healing for yourself too. As I said, it's a scenario where everyone wins.

So, the start isn't a jump headfirst into the deep end of the pool. It's an intentional move into a space where you allow yourself to be seen bit by bit. And while even baby steps in that direction might seem seriously daunting right now, there truly is nothing like being seen – being loved, appreciated, and valued for who you are. All of you – including the parts you thought were too ugly to share.

The truth is: there's beauty in those ashes. Find the first glimmer and keep digging, keep sharing, keep raising your voice. You'll find that what you've been hiding in the dark is a treasure more valuable than you ever imagined.

CHAPTER 11

My Secret: I Don't Think I'm Good Enough

The Truth: I Don't Have to Prove Anything to Anyone

I spent the majority of my life as a people-pleaser who was trying to prove I was good enough and smart enough for people to like, love, and accept me. I couldn't understand why I often found myself surrounded by toxic people and stuck in toxic environments. I always figured that giving and people-pleasing was the way I showed good people that I was good, valuable, and worthy, too.

But it never worked. It did not earn me the love and respect of anyone at all.

I ultimately learned this secret about people-pleasers and givers: we attract takers.

That's because givers, overperformers, and overachievers are often operating from a toxic perspective. We're not bending over backward and jumping through hoops for everyone out of goodwill and generosity; we're doing it because we're trying to make ourselves feel better; we're trying to fill our own voids. So, we figure that we can prove just how valuable and worthy we are by giving to others the things we need in hopes that they'll see our value and give back to us.

We don't realize it, but that's how we become magnets for people who enjoy receiving from us without feeling any need to reciprocate. Because as toxic as we are in our giving, they are equally as toxic in their taking. So, as long as we are pouring, they feel just fine receiving. That is how we end up surrounded by the complete opposite of what we'd hoped to attract.

That's Now How Any of This Works

When we consistently dishonor ourselves by giving what we don't have, people start to believe that we're ok with just scraping to get by while we help them meet their needs. To us, it feels diminishing and disrespectful, but they're just playing by the rules we set. They learned from us that we're ok with an empty cup, because we rarely – if ever – attend to our own refilling.

We were never meant to give to others from a place of deficit, and we weren't intended to delegate our refilling to them, either. It's our responsibility to make sure our cups are filled. So filled, in fact, that what others receive from us comes from our overflow – not our last remaining drops. We forget that as much as we want to require others to love us in deeds and not just in words, we have to do the same for ourselves.

We need to sever the ties between our sense of our "goodness" and "worthiness" and our perception of how well we treat everyone else and spend more time assessing how good we've been to ourselves each day. Our worth and our value should be measured by the words we speak to ourselves rather than those spoken by people who don't have the authority to make the assessment.

Pushing Through Is for Delivering Babies – Not for Mental Health

For far too long, we've defined strength as our ability to function well in a state of lack – and I'm not talking about money. I mean that emotionally and mentally, we have been functioning without seeing to it that our needs are met. The fallacy is in our belief that because we're still able to perform at a higher capacity than most others – even when we're in a deficit – we're "strong".

As long as we believe this to be true, we will never see that making ourselves a priority is important. We'll continue being tricked into thinking that taking care of ourselves first is selfish. But think about it – can you effectively perform the Heimlich if your air is choked off and you can't breathe? As much as you might want the person you're helping to live, you're dying in the process. Once they start to breathe again, what kind of condition will you be in?

Yes, we've done a great job of crafting personas that make us look like we're better on the outside than we feel inside. And I don't mean putting on a brave face during difficult times, I'm talking about the way we step into entirely new personalities that deceive people into believing that the parts of us that are screaming in pain don't exist at all. We do this because, in addition to seeking external validation, we also don't want to be seen as weak or as failures.

The problem with this kind of strength is that it consumes you and brings depression, anxiety, and other mental health conditions along with it. Now, I certainly leave plenty of room for the understanding that mental health conditions can be the result of chemical and hormonal imbalances in our bodies, but I also recognize that some of them also result from unhealed pain. Toxic strength has made us believe that "pushing through" is the way to reach better days – and sometimes it does. But more often than not, "pushing through" simply wears us out and makes us feel worse over time.

It's like trying to close a gash with gauze. We have these deep emotional injuries that we need to attend to, but because we don't want people to know that we're injured and hurting, we simply cover them up, hoping that by hiding them, no one will see that we're bleeding. We do everything we can to keep people focused on the persona we've crafted so they won't see the parts of us that are gangrenous and dying.

Now, I can tell you firsthand that the gauze works. I've been at low points – in tears prior to meetings or crying on my way to work because I knew the toxic mess I was about to walk into – but at the appointed time, I dried my eyes, fixed my make-up, squared my shoulders and walked in like the baddie everyone knew me to be. I smiled and greeted each person like the day was another one of God's best and brightest, and no one had any idea that I was emotionally and mentally "bleeding out".

And while that was a great disguise, the hiding was adding insult to my injuries. I felt empty, resentful, and bitter because no one saw me – no, because I wouldn't let anyone see me. The parts of me that wanted to scream, "I AM NOT OK!!" were trapped inside and taking their anger out on me, trying to claw their way out. The inner turmoil was real, but I didn't dare let it show externally.

People thought I was strong, but I was fighting a losing battle. I was hiding depression, anxiety, and paranoia – and they were all getting worse by the day. I arrived at a point where I could no longer "push through", and I finally had to deal with everything I was secretly carrying.

U Gotta Love Yourself

Let me give you an ugly truth: You're not ok just because you haven't fallen apart yet. You've been "strong" up to now, but your arms are shaking. Your body is begging to be released from the pain and trauma it's storing, yet you continue drowning out its cries with more work and more responsibility. When you submerge yourself in busyness, it's easy to ignore the signals your body is giving you to let you know that a meltdown or a blowup is on the way. And it won't be until you're recovering from a crisis that you look back and realize, *I should have seen that coming.*

We have an urgent need for self-care, but we routinely misinterpret what that term means. It's more than taking a day to get a massage or going for your weekly manicure and pedicure. Those activities are great, but they do little to address the way we feel about how the world has treated us. The best self-care you can give yourself is to sit and be honest about what you feel and why – and then to allow yourself to release those feelings. This is an act of care because it allows you to be honest and heal intentionally.

Healing can take place with time, but time will not heal your wounds. That's because most often, instead of using the time to heal, we teach ourselves coping strategies that will help us live with the pain. Once we're used to it, we forget we've been injured, and we think we no longer need help.

This is why you can return from trips and getaways feeling as lousy as you did before you left. It's also why you can return to sadness so quickly after a shopping spree or a night out with friends. Those moments were just temporary escapes from the weights you carry. When you return, you simply pick them all back up, put the "I'm ok" smile back on your face, and go back to trudging through life with your trauma and pain on your shoulders.

Get Somewhere and Sit Down

It's so difficult for many of us to choose silence – to opt for stillness and quietness. To allow our most painful thoughts to float to the surface of our minds so we can see them, feel them, and release them – to admit to ourselves that we may never get that apology, we may never recover the time we lost, and we may never retrieve the innocence that was taken from us. The people who hurt us may never do anything to make things right with us, but we cannot allow their inaction to continue impacting our lives. We must, at some point, attend to ourselves, so we can deactivate their power over us.

The loudest voice we must deal with is our own. We're so self-critical! There's no one harder on us than we are on ourselves. We are the ones cracking the whip every morning, forcing ourselves to execute each day flawlessly. Our voices are the ones that replay and evaluate the comments we make throughout the day; we're the ones who issue shame and guilt when we don't say just the right thing at just the right time. It's our voice that questions our every move and makes us doubt our decision making, and it is our voice that makes us feel insecure in our relationships.

It's not always the world that's telling us we're not worthy of love and respect. If we're honest, our need for validation stems from the inability to tell ourselves that we are worthy. We think we have something to prove to the world – when what we're really trying to do is prove something to ourselves.

We toss around the phrase, "The only person I'm in competition with is me," but I wonder how many of us are making that declaration with the mindset of self-improvement versus self-criticism. In other words, how many of us are actually saying "I'm trying to prove to myself that I'm really as good as I pretend to be."

We've got to give ourselves grace. I know we hear that a lot, but we don't truly take it in and apply it the way we should. Giving ourselves grace means refusing to second guess ourselves. It means using our strength to catch the unkind words we think and speak to ourselves and stop them in their tracks. It's giving ourselves the validation we desire, because we know we're worthy of it.

Think about it – out of all that has been created over the billions of years since the "Big Bang", you exist – on purpose and by design. Astrophysicist Neil deGrasse Tyson once pointed out that the odds of any one of us being alive are nearly incomprehensible. He said that if every possible combination of DNA resulted in a person, the world would see approximately 10^{30} potential humans come to life. That's 10 followed by thirty zeros!

Yet, most of these people will never exist. So, this is our value: the fact that we are here – that we beat the odds. Out of a quadrillion-quadrillion possibilities for human life, ours came into being.

There's nothing more to prove. Continuing to prove that you're valuable is just an exercise in futility. The people who are committed to misunderstanding you will keep on doing so, and there's nothing you can do about that. The only thing you can do is to keep yourself from internalizing their misunderstanding. It is not your fault that they don't see your value. Don't waste valuable time in your life trying to convince the inconvincible. You'll make yourself crazy.

Take "The Out"

Acknowledging that we have no need for toxic giving or people-pleasing opens the door to offloading – or rejecting altogether – people and situations that add toxicity to our lives. Maya Angelou is famously quoted as saying, "When someone shows you who they are, believe them the first time. They know themselves much better than you do." While the saying is wildly popular, we often do the opposite. Instead of taking her suggestion, we dismiss the reality we see in favor of the potential we do not see. I'm not saying that people don't have potential or that they cannot change. Rather, it means that we shouldn't be blind to the reality of what's in front of us.

Before you can repair anything, you must acknowledge how broken it is. That's the only way you can accurately determine what it will take to fix the problem – or whether issue can be resolved at all. Many of us, however, become enamored with what we believe someone or something can be, without fully acknowledging what it currently is. As a result, we miss the fact that we're starting from DOA – dead on arrival – and we're trying to breathe life into something that took its last breath a long time ago.

Our new definition of strength gives us permission to take a step back before we jump in with our heart or our help. It lets us pause to assess whether the person or the environment is worthy of us, and it lets us refuse to get involved when we discover that what we're being asked to do will take more from us than it will give back.

We often find ourselves drained by toxic people and environments because as people-pleasers, we don't ask the right questions before diving into the rabbit hole of working with them. Then, even when we recognize that we're constantly feeling drained, bitter, resentful, or even hateful toward the person or the work, we still remain in those situations. Whether it's because we believe there's some hidden goodness within that toxic person, or because we're clinging to the hope that things will improve "any day now," we refuse to call a time of death on our involvement and walk away.

The best thing we can do for ourselves, though, is to "take the out".

I once said this to a girlfriend who was seeing a man who'd ghosted her for several months. Though he had plenty of flowery compliments when he finally resurfaced, all he'd ever offer was a bunch of circular talk and vagueness any time she'd ask why he'd disappeared. She felt tempted to ignore it all and take him back because she really liked spending time with him, even though they had only talked for a few months before he vanished. My advice to her was simple: *take the out*.

He had been gone for so long that she had already moved on from thinking and talking about him. So, for her, taking the out meant letting the relationship stay exactly where he'd left it. In doing so, she'd be honoring the red flags that were waving right in front of her, and rather than allowing herself to be caught up in what was sure to be more of an "entanglement" than a relationship, she could take the exit he had offered her when he ghosted her.

Of course, this principle doesn't apply only to toxic people; it can be used in any environment. After my breakdown, I made the decision to walk away from that toxic organization. I had overstayed my welcome. I'd been stubbornly clinging to my vision of how I thought things should be, while ignoring the clear signs from God that my time there had come to an end.

I, too, was willing to ignore the red flags waving right in front of me, because I was being driven by the need to prove that I was strong enough to handle anything. I wanted to show that I wasn't someone who could be easily walked over. But in doing so, I once again lost sight of the most important truth: *I don't have to prove anything to anyone.*

With that realization, I was able to fully release the entire matter. I took the out. When I announced my resignation, it was with joy and excitement

– not only for the new chapter that was before me, but also because of the peace I felt after making a decision that put my care and wellness first. Instead of bagging up those feelings and dragging them further down a toxic path, I'd chosen to put them down and make a decision in my favor, finally.

That day, as I walked down the sidewalk and away from that office for the last time, I felt a profound sense of freedom from the weight I had been carrying. I felt like I was floating! I couldn't help but smile. Yes, I was happy it was over, but more than that, I was proud of myself. All the battles I had fought to feel validated had led nowhere. But standing up for myself? That felt so good.

Honesty, The Best Policy

I was able to release the secret that I didn't feel like I was "good enough" when I started to be honest about the person I was trying to be good enough for – me. I realized that I needed the validation to drown out the inside voices that kept me feeling like I was flawed, like I always could have and should have done better. They made me think that those flaws were what everyone "out there" focused on – that they'd forget all about everything I'd accomplished and all the good I'd done just to focus on what I was unable or unwilling to do.

Once I began telling myself that the value I hold is based on the value I assign to myself, things began to change. People's opinions of me no longer held the weight they once did – especially once I realized that many of them are pretending, too – just like I was. I gave myself the grace and room to heal from feeling that I'd been rejected because I wasn't good enough. At the end of it all, I realized that the many times I thought I was being rejected, God was actually protecting me and opening the doors to my next opportunities.

There are two things we must remember when we fall into the trap of feeling we must prove our value to other people. One, it is possible that they're not meant to see our value – as the saying goes, beauty is in the eye of the beholder. No matter how hard we try to convince them, some people will never validate us in the way we desire them to. The second thing we must remember is that we teach people how to value us based on the value we assign to ourselves. If we treat ourselves as valueless, they're going to follow our lead.

We demonstrate our self-value by how we treat ourselves on a daily basis. It's not enough to engage in surface-level self-care. We must go deeper. Our self-care should reflect our active commitment to healing our trauma and releasing painful secrets.

I now recognize that I am the one who gets to determine my value – and so do you. You, too, have the chance to decide what's written on your price tag. Just know that whatever you put there, the world will honor. They may not want to "pay" what it takes to have access to you – the authentic you – but they will have to respect what's there.

Letting go of the need to prove yourself is the ultimate act of self-liberation, and it begins the moment you start valuing yourself for who you are and not for what you can do.

The truth is, you're enough. You've always been enough – regardless of what anyone else sees or thinks. Once you stop trying to convince the wrong people of your value, you'll create space for the right ones to show up and honor you as you deserve.

The great news is: YOU get to set the standard. You get to teach the world how to treat you by showing up boldly and unapologetically for yourself.

That's real freedom.

CHAPTER 12

My Secret: My Heart is Broken
The Truth: I Forgive You

There's a saying that goes, "Holding on to anger is like drinking poison and expecting the other person to die." Anger, offense, and hatred are the most toxic of human emotions, yet we often hold on to them like they're security blankets. Grief, while it may not be as toxic as hatred, offense, and anger can be, can become toxic when we hold onto it for too long or when we ignore it and allow it to go uncontrolled and unsupervised.

Certainly, there's no way to avoid tragedy, loss, or heartbreak, but there are healthy ways to deal with them. And while we may not control how often or how long we experience pain, we can prevent ourselves from harboring them and allowing them to eat away at us slowly.

Forgiveness just might be the worst "f-word" you'll find in this book – but for many people it is as insulting as the actual f-word. Forgiving someone who hurt you is not easy to do. It can feel like you're letting them off the hook, when what you really want is for them to feel the same pain and heartbreak you're feeling. And because they're not, it's easier to hold on to unforgiveness as a way to remind them that they're still bad people in your eyes.

But it doesn't work. All unforgiveness does is delay our healing. Most times we don't realize it, but when we hold on to heartbreak and grief for too long, resentment and bitterness set in, and we start looking for someone to blame for why we're hurting so badly. Sometimes we blame ourselves. Sometimes we blame another person, an institution, or God. Our hearts crave a target for our anger and loss, and without one, moving forward can feel nearly impossible.

It's true – forgiveness is complicated. It doesn't come with the instant gratification that revenge seems to promise. And if we're honest, that's what most of us want. We desire revenge more than wholeness. Most of us think we'd feel better if the person who hurt us could experience the same pain we're feeling from what they did to us, but we wouldn't. Certainly, we might enjoy seeing them squirm for the moment, but the fact will remain that we're not healed. Even if the person who hurt you dropped dead tomorrow, you'd still have to deal with your broken heart.

How Do You Mend a Broken Heart?

A big part of my healing journey was coming to the understanding that I held a lot of anger, resentment, and distrust against God. So many times, I'd found myself asking, How could He let this happen to me? Of course, my inability to believe that He loved and cared about me contributed to the grudge I held against him, because I wanted to know how God could love me and allow me to experience so much pain.

Even after I began to understand the nature of His love for me, I still found it hard to let go of some of that deep resentment I held, and I had a hard time expressing love, honor, and praise to Him in the way I desired. I'm not sure when it hit me that I needed to forgive God, but I came to see that it was me who needed to clear the air between us.

We hear so much about God forgiving us, we never think about our need to forgive Him – to release the resentment and bitterness we're feeling toward Him because He didn't unfold our lives the way we thought He should have. Maybe He didn't heal you or a loved one the way you thought He would, or perhaps He didn't save your marriage like you'd hoped. Or maybe you'd placed all your faith in what you believed He was going to do – and it didn't happen.

The list could go on and on, but when we're grieving heartbreak, the first person we usually point the finger at is God. Because if He loves us and is fully in control, then it would seem that He had the power to answer our prayers when we asked, the way we asked – and simply chose not to. In our grief, we don't see any sort of divine orchestration. We're unable to comprehend that the "no" we received from Him could have been part of a bigger picture. All we can see is that we didn't get what we thought we needed from Him.

The best thing that could happen for me was the discovery of God's love for me. Once I understood that He wasn't holding a grudge against me, I was able to get beyond the idea that He wanted to harm me or that He was ok with my being harmed. I didn't have explanations for the heartbreak and grief I'd experienced, but this awareness allowed me to begin releasing my anger toward Him.

I admitted to Him that that I didn't understand why He'd allowed my heart to be broken, and that I wanted to heal and find the strength to trust Him again. I figured that, as the God of the universe, He could handle my hesitation and uncertainty. And I found that He just wanted me to be willing to surrender my grief and my broken heart to Him, so he could heal me. He wanted me to see that it is safe to release my negative feelings to Him and receive – not just acknowledge – the love He has for me.

Forgiving God helped close the distance I felt between us. It's one thing to know you're loved; it's an entirely different thing to believe it and receive that love. It really made a difference in our relationship. It also pushed me to take a long look at forgiving myself. I hadn't realized it, but I was also harboring resentment and unforgiveness against me, too.

There were many toxic people I'd allowed in my life and so many harmful places I'd allowed myself to get stuck in. I didn't just blame the people who'd hurt me, though. I held myself responsible for putting myself in the position to be mistreated in the first place. I was the one who didn't listen to my intuition – or God – when the red flags started popping up and waving.

There were so many painful periods of my life that would have been much shorter if I had acted on what I knew a year or two into them. Instead, I have wasted 5 years, or 10 years on relationships and projects that I knew were dead in the water after just a couple years of being involved. I blamed myself for being foolish enough to think that bad situations would get better – or at least become more tolerable – over time. But of course, that never happened.

So, I lost the ability to trust myself, because I believed I made bad choices – especially when it came to areas of my life where I really wanted things to succeed. When it came time to heal my heart, one of the first places I had to start was with me. I had to forgive myself for the decisions I made that weren't in my best interest. I also had to forgive myself for adopting the belief that I can't be trusted to make good decisions when it comes to my heart.

Some of those bad choices were made out of fear – of being alone, of starting over, or of losing something or someone I loved. Others were made because I didn't know how to use my voice to advocate for myself. I had to forgive myself for being unable to make good choices when I was afraid. Fear makes you do things that aren't rational and don't make sense for your long-term benefit. It causes you to react to what's happening from a place of emotion, rather than responding from a place of calmness and logic.

And when you've been abused and you haven't fully healed, your ability to make choices for yourself is crippled because you're still grappling with the events that took certain choices away from you in the first place.

To heal, we must extend some grace to ourselves, especially if our ability to choose was corrupted very early in life. We must not only forgive the young woman who was doing the best she could with the decision-making and coping skills she had at the time, we also have to forgive ourselves for being so hard on her and making her feel as though she wasn't worthy of our patience and our trust.

We have to stop beating ourselves up over the heartbreak we caused ourselves and calling it "taking responsibility". Certainly, we should take ownership of who and what we allow to enter and remain in our lives, but accountability doesn't mean that we get to continuously beat ourselves up and second-guess ourselves forever. Accountability means owning your part in the mess you made, forgiving yourself, and giving yourself permission to heal and move forward.

Even after forgiving God and myself, I still had to grapple with the idea of forgiving the people who hurt me. Since I'm being honest, I'll tell you I didn't want to. I felt as though I had a right to be offended and to continue holding on to those grudges. If there was any real blame to be placed, here was where I could point the finger at facts and say, "You did this to me."

Yet scripture says not only are we to love our neighbors as ourselves; it also says (paraphrasing) that if we forgive, our heavenly Father will forgive us, but if we do not forgive, our Father will not forgive us, either (Matthew 6:9-14). And when Jesus gave us the model prayer, He said we're to ask God to "forgive us our debts as we forgive our debtors". Those debts aren't credit cards and car notes – that word "debt" refers to ethical and moral wrongdoings. Put simply – we must forgive if we want to be forgiven.

Holding on to unforgiveness is a form of self-harm. It's choosing to keep experiencing pain, because as long as we're hurting, we can justify pointing the finger at the people who caused our pain.

The problem with that, however, is that most times, the people we're refusing to forgive either don't know we're still angry or don't care. While we're lying awake at night, replaying what we should have said or what we should have done in the moment (sometimes years after it's happened), the person we're mad at is likely turning over in their bed, pulling the covers to their ears, and drooling their way into the next morning.

In other words, we're the only ones who pay for our inability to forgive the people who hurt us. By now it should be clear that I understand what it feels like to be hurt deeply by people who had been granted unrestricted access to your entire heart. And I can still tell you that it is possible to forgive them. It's not easy, but it is possible. And it is necessary.

There's absolutely nothing we can do to make someone feel bad for what they did to us, nor can we force an apology from them. The sooner we accept that, the easier it will be to let go of offense. If we refuse, the anger, depression, and anxiety that come with allowing unforgiveness to fester – whether actively or subconsciously – affect us, not them.

Forgiving is Selfish

Remember, in our new definition of strength, we are no longer carrying what doesn't belong to us. So, when you forgive someone, you are not handing them a "get out of jail free" card for what they did to you. You're simply refusing to carry the weight of their actions. It doesn't matter if they ever own up to it or apologize. It doesn't even matter if you tell them you're forgiving them.

You can forgive someone even if you never plan to speak to them again (or if you're unable to). Your ability to forgive does not hinge on their ability to apologize. It is a selfish act that snatches control and your ability to heal out of the hands of the people who hurt you and gives it back to you. To put it plainly, forgiveness is for you.

One of the things we must remember is that we cannot hold people accountable who don't want to be. And we cannot make them take responsibility if they don't see that they're responsible. We can only control ourselves and what we choose to allow into our lives.

And finally, if there's an apology you need to make, do it. The flip side to the coin of forgiveness is offering an apology when you've hurt someone. A lot of us are carrying around hidden grief and pain because we know we need to go to someone and own up to what we did. It's another humbling act, indeed, but it's necessary, too. If we're going to use strength properly, let's use it to carry what *does* belong to us. Even if you don't believe your apology will be accepted, offer it. Take direct ownership of your actions (saying, "I'm sorry I…" is a good start) and then leave the other person to do whatever they desire to do with what you've offered.

Again, we're not doing any of this for the responses we believe we should get. We're doing this to be free, as another form of self-care. We're being selfish in the healthiest way possible. We're giving ourselves a gift called forgiveness and we're opening the doors to the healing and wholeness we deserve.

CHAPTER 13

My Secret: Maybe God's Forgotten About Me

The Truth: God Loves Me—Really

It took a long time for me to realize that God's affection toward me wasn't demonstrated by His doing what I wanted or always working things out in my favor. I also had to learn that my suffering didn't mean He'd abandoned me or forgotten about me, and He wasn't withholding the answers to my prayers because He was displeased with me.

Still, I couldn't understand why God would allow me to endure physical abuse. Stuff like that wasn't part of my familial tapestry. In fact, I had always been the type to say, "I wish a [expletive] would!" any time I heard or read a story about a woman being abused. That is, until a [expletive] actually did.

Mike Tyson is quoted as saying "Everybody has a plan until they get punched in the face." Now, I didn't get hit quite like that, but the sentiment remains true – everybody thinks they know how they will react until they're faced with the offense personally. While I was enduring the emotional turmoil of loss and abuse, I couldn't see that I was being prepared for a life in which I was called to serve women from all kinds of backgrounds. I didn't know it, but God was using those painful seasons to take me off my self-appointed pedestal and place me in the position to know true compassion for those who had endured divorce, abuse, and loss. He took me from feeling like I'd handle things so expertly to understanding that I am just like them – that when faced with these issues in real life, I'd react no differently than they had.

As painful as those times were, they were not to harm me – they were necessary for my life's purpose. Of course, I couldn't see it at the time – through the lens of my own pain, but today, after connecting with and talking with thousands of women, I can empathize with those who are in abusive situations they don't know how to escape. I can feel the pain of the woman whose world was upended by unexpected loss. I know what it feels like to lose everything and not know what the future will hold or whether there's a future at all.

I also know what it's like to bounce back from every bad day – every horrible season – I've ever faced. For sure, it wasn't easy, and I know I made many mistakes along the way. But I can say that I know what's it's like to go from struggling to afford a $15 field trip to experiencing financial freedom.

They say that our testimonies come from our tests, and as cliché as it sounds, it's not untrue. The seasons of suffering that we endure are purposeful. They build strength. The challenge for many of us, though, is that we believe we display strength when we can make people believe we're not affected by our pain – or that we're not suffering at all. But I beg to differ. There are seasons where you will come out of the fight looking 100% like what you've been through.

And that's ok.

Our strength isn't marked by how indestructible we can appear to be. Nor does it reflect how well we can carry our baggage from one crisis to the next. Spiritual strength is built just like physical strength. There are burdens we must carry for a season that can, at times, make us feel as though we have gone past the point of exhaustion. But our strength is built in those moments of testing and endurance. And because as we're pushed to our limits, we develop new muscles and strengthen the ones we already have.

So, the saying, "God won't put more on you than you can bear," isn't the whole story. He definitely puts more on us than we think we can bear, but He knows our limits and He knows the strength He desires to build in us. He's definitely the master trainer. The weights we carry are intended to prepare us for the next set – for the more challenging work out.

But those weights aren't meant to be dragged through our lives. They're intended to develop us for a season and prepare us for the complex tasks of our purpose that lie ahead. Our periods of trials, failures, and suffering show us what we're made of and let us see the fruit that blossom from the seeds of what God put in us. His goal is to develop us into people who can be trusted to take what life throws at them and transform it into a victory story.

So, What's Love Got to Do with It?

I'm glad you asked.

When I was going through my toughest times, the enemy would often speak to me and make me believe that there was something wrong with me or that God was punishing me. That evil voice insisted that I was suffering because I was a bad person and because I failed to meet God's standards. He wanted me to believe that because God wasn't rescuing me, He wasn't going to – that I was forgotten, unloved, and ignored.

So, I found myself trying to be perfect for God, just like I'd tried to be perfect for everyone else, to earn his approval. I tried to learn all the "right" ways to pray, and I tried to be perfect with reading scripture and church attendance. Even as I began preaching on a regular basis, I found myself trying to craft perfect sermons because I believed that was the standard God required of me.

When I rededicated my life to Him, I thought the process of transformation would be instantaneous – once I gave my life over to him fully, my days would be full of spiritual bliss. Boy was I wrong! As with any part of life, this walk is a process, and it's not the good days that build your faith or make you stronger. It's not the joyous moments you have in church nor the times when you feel most content and happy with your life that mold you into who you're created to be.

It's those periods when all you seem to do is fast, pray, cry, and pray some more for God's help, which shove you into your real self – the self He crafted and destined you to be. Those seasons are where character is built – where you get to see what you're made of, as well as which traits still need to be cultivated.

As the ultimate Good Father, God knows His kids – especially us hard-headed ones. He knows that telling us to go exercise won't be enough. To build the muscles we'll need in the coming years of our lives, He knows we'll only build the strength we'll need through experience. It's the only way we'll know without doubt that we can win when we face adversity.

It's kind of like David when he was facing Goliath. As others doubted whether he could handle his opponent, he reflected on what he'd previously been through to remind himself and his doubters that he had everything he needed to be victorious, even though he'd never fought this particular enemy before. He recalled that throughout his life, while he'd been left to tend to his father's flock of sheep, he'd already tussled with lions and bears that sought to steal what belonged to him. Those memories of triumph gave him the confidence to look at this new formidable obstacle and say, I can beat that, too.

And that's what we must remember. Nothing we go through is wasted. The strength that's being developed in us isn't for withstanding a life where we're entrapped by every bad thing that's ever happened to us. Instead, our seasons of suffering and periods of trial should leave us with lessons learned and with new tactics and strategies to deploy when the next challenge rears its head.

I've been saying that our strength lies in knowing what not to carry, so we've got to release the weight of feeling like God doesn't love us or care about our circumstance just because we don't like the one we're in. If we could look back and see just how far we've come and the many things we've overcome, and if we can allow ourselves to heal from the residual pain of the fights we've endured, we'll see that while what we went through may not have *felt* good, it was *for* our good.

The thing is, you cannot allow those seasons of your life – nor the voice of the enemy – to make you believe that your tough times reflect some sort of revenge God is getting on you, or that He doesn't love you. Because the truth is, He loves us all so much He was willing to sacrifice what he loved most – His Son.

His Strongest Soldiers

So, God's been teaching you how to trust Him more deeply. He's been building a faith in you that wouldn't rely on your feelings or on visible evidence, but one which rests on the unshakable truth of His love. He was showing you that you weren't alone, even when you felt most isolated, and He was proving to you that the pain you've endured wasn't for nothing; it's the foundation for the strength He's developing in you.

Our faith gets stronger when we realize that just like He's allowed us to overcome every obstacle we've endured so far, He's going to take care of the ones that will arise in the future, as well. He designed us with purpose so He can't forget about us. We are part of His intricate plan. When we finally acknowledge that He – as the master orchestrator – knows the plans he has for us and is looking at our lives through the timeless lens of eternity, we can begin to trust that He has everything under control and that He can be trusted to make sure we'll have what we need when we need it.

God handles many of us "strong" ones this way because we often believe we're the ones in control. But the strength we need can't come from our own efforts, or else we'll conclude that our strength is greater than His. But His strength comes from surrendering, from letting go of the need to control, and from allowing ourselves to be held by a God who won't let us be plucked out of His hands. It's the kind of strength that allows us to move forward even when we don't have all the answers. It's the strength that keeps us believing, even when our hearts feel weary. It's the courage to trust that God is for us, even when life is against us.

That's why I know now, without a doubt, that God has never, ever forgotten about me. And He hasn't forgotten about you, either. He's been there through every heartbreak, every disappointment, and every dark season, whispering His love into the very places where we've felt most broken. He's been weaving beauty out of our pain, crafting purpose from our struggles, and leading us toward a future that far exceeds anything we could have imagined.

Any time we feel lost, abandoned, or overlooked, we must remember: God's silence is not His absence, and His timing is not neglect. He is ever-present. We must trust that, even when it's hard. Believe that He loves you, even when you can't see it. And know that He has a plan for your life that is good. A plan that is filled with hope, with purpose, and an ending He's well aware of.

When we look at all the things He's brought us through and saved us from, it becomes quite apparent that He's never really let us down. He's just worked things out differently than we desired, because He could see a bigger picture. In trusting God, we must learn to listen for His voice, especially when we think He's not paying attention. He is, though, and He's got everything under control. Our job is to trust Him and find peace in knowing that he loves His kids.

Yes, even us.

CHAPTER 14

My Secret: It's All on Me

The Truth: I Don't Have to If I Don't Want To

I'm not sure who made "no" a bad word, but it's not. In fact, it is a complete sentence all by itself.

Still, we often feel bad when we use it – perhaps because it feels like we're letting someone down. Or maybe it's because our inner voice tends to speak up just before we say no and remind us that others might feel bad if we do. So, we avoid saying no. We either soften the blow with excuses or lies, or – more commonly – we say yes even though we don't want to.

But what if we just said,

"No."

"I'd rather not."

"I don't want to."

"I'd prefer not to."

"Not just nah, h*ll nah!"

Well – perhaps the last option was a bit over the top for some, but my point remains just the same. You can say no unapologetically! The problem for many of us is that somewhere along the line we were made to feel as though saying no was mean or inconsiderate of the plights of others.

But if I could, I'd like to suggest that the word "no" is one of the highest forms of self-care. It is a boundary setter, and it honors your values and your needs. It really should be a word we respect more – but because it's often viewed from the perspective of being denied something, we miss the fact that the word no can give much more than it takes away.

In saying no, we close doors to the things that don't suit us, and we open doors to the opportunities that are perfect for us. Most of the time, those opportunities are bigger and better than the ones we said no to.

But instead of focusing on the inflow of the good, the great, and the amazing that can come to us when we say no, we focus more on the possible negative outcomes – the hurt feelings, the delay of gratification, the rejection. We project the feelings we've experienced from being told no onto other people and assume they will feel the same way when we say no to them. So, we're not really worried about their feelings, we're worried about them feeling the way we would feel if we were in their shoes!

Telling someone – or yourself – no isn't inherently bad. Like anything else, the logic and reason behind the response is what matters. When it's used to protect your peace and to enforce healthy boundaries, it is liberating and empowering. On the other hand, when you're afraid to say no because you're afraid of the fallout, it's toxic.

Just Say No

On my journey to redefine strength, I discovered that "no" was an extremely hard word for me to say. I felt as though I didn't have the right to use it, as if uttering it would disqualify me from being loved and feeling wanted. Saying no also felt like non-compliance. It symbolized going against the rules and doing something I wasn't supposed to.

It pained me to say no. Any time I did, I'd ruminate over it for days or weeks, worried whether the person I'd denied really meant it when they'd said, "It's ok." To avoid this feeling, I'd end up saying yes to doing things I knew I didn't want to do – or couldn't do. And I'd be the one walking away from the request feeling bad – upset and annoyed with myself for not saying no.

I learned that my inability – or unwillingness – to say no was at the root of my self-sacrificing. It communicated that I didn't see myself as a priority and signaled that I was okay with making myself miserable – repeatedly to keep the peace or make others happy. But the word "no" actually released me from unwanted obligation and freed me to be fully present when I could be and when I wanted to be. It allowed me to protect myself from overuse, and it returned to me the right to rest when I needed to.

Give Yourself Permission to Be Selfish

While it might be easy to conceptualize the power of "no", the challenge is putting it into practice in everyday life. Especially if you, like me, aren't one of the people who can say "no" and walk off as if they had just read you the weather. If you feel uncomfortable – perhaps, even unworthy – when it comes to saying no, putting it to use will take intentionality and practice.

The first step in this part of the journey is understanding that saying no does not detract from your value or your worthiness. It does not reflect lack, nor does it indicate weakness. Instead, the ability to say no reflects a keen awareness of self – of your capacity and your bandwidth; it allows for self-advocacy and the enforcement of healthy boundaries. In other words, saying no helps *you* look out for *you*.

The next step is realizing that even if you say yes 100 times, someone will be upset about the one time you say no. There simply is no way to make everyone happy with you all the time. And, truthfully, it's not your job to make them happy. You have no control over how others will react to the decisions you make. So, as long as you're making decisions that are in line with your values and aren't harmful to you or to others, make the decision and stand "ten toes down" on it. If someone is unhappy with that, it's ok. They'll get over it – and if they don't, their reaction should tell you plenty about them that you'll need to consider and remember in the future.

Thirdly, don't allow people to weaponize guilt. There's no reason you should be made to feel bad for taking care of or standing up for yourself. If there are people around you who do this, keep your "no" as short as possible. The more you debate the "why" of your response, the worse they'll try to make you feel. It may take a little effort and a little preplanning of what you might say – or better yet, what you won't say – to make sure they understand that standing up for yourself isn't a slight to them. But make it clear that you are still saying no.

Finally, as you empower yourself by saying no to things you don't want to participate in, you'll need to understand that there will be days when you'll have to decide where you'll excel and where you'll fail. By that, I mean sometimes saying no will be strategic. Saying no to that extra project at work might mean that today you fail as the "star employee", but you excel as "mom" because you made it home early enough to spend some extra time with your family. Conversely, saying "no" to movies with the kids tonight, because you need to say yes to an important task for your business, might mean that you've got grumpy kids in the moment, but security for them in the future.

Ultimately, saying no is a demonstration of love to ourselves. When used well, it teaches others that our views of love and respect do not include self-harm and self-neglect. It lets them know that we choose to interact with the world from a place of self-love, wholeness, and overflow.

Get Somebody Else to Do It

Saying "no" is the admission that we have no desire to carry the weight of the world on our shoulders any longer. We recognize that our strength is primarily for us, and this means the weights we're carrying for others can be released. I'm not saying that you shouldn't care about what the people around you are going through or how they feel. I am saying that if it's not your weight to carry around, don't. You can have empathy about their predicament without taking ownership of it.

Yes, you can care too much. This is especially true for those of us who are empathic and emotionally intelligent. If we're honest, we'll admit that we often take "being there" for people too far. We're not just there for them; we're in it with them. Rather than standing on the shore and throwing a life raft, we've jumped into the rip tide, too, and now everybody's sinking.

Being the one who'll give someone the clothes off your back is only a good thing when you have something else to wear. We commend people who sacrifice in this way, and while there are times when this sort of selfless generosity is warranted, we can't do that with every person we meet and in every needful situation we find ourselves in. If we're constantly giving from a limited supply, we end up with nothing!

And that's where many of us find ourselves when we realize that we're tired of being everyone's go-to and safety net. When I hit this point, I came to a tough realization: I was emotionally over-invested in matters that really weren't my business at all simply because I couldn't say no. I'd been worried about how other people would find jobs, pay rent, and take care of their children. I was afraid they'd think I had let them down. I was attempting to protect folks who didn't belong to me and trying to control the matters that were influencing their lives.

None of the things I'd been stressing about in the months leading up to my breakdown had anything to do with me – not one thing. I kept saying, "I just want to make sure they're ok." Meanwhile, no one was as stressed for me as I was for them. And that's not a dig at them; I had simply gone overboard. I was more concerned about what they would do and how they would manage their lives, and I completely stopped tending to my own.

Meanwhile, my house was a wreck, I was forgetting about and missing appointments, I wasn't sleeping well, and I was a weepy, cranky mess. My anxiety was sky high, and my mood was extremely low. It was hard work getting out of bed on the days I was able to. Things were out of my control, and I was becoming angrier about it by the day.

For someone who has a Type A personality, is accustomed to being in control, and who generally gets what she wants, "out of control" is a terrible place to be. We're used to a particular formula, in which any time we are added to chaotic situations, order appears. When we can't make that happen, we don't just accept that the situation isn't fixable, we double down and try harder. It seems implausible to us that we can't fix everything we put our hands on or our minds to.

My turning point came with the realization of an important fact. I am not in control, nor do I want to be. Much like the main character in the movie Bruce Almighty, I quickly discovered that God's job is much too much for me to handle. I am not equipped to micromanage the lives of multiple people, and I have absolutely no influence over the external forces acting on their lives. I was handling my own life poorly, and it was evident that I was in no position to handle anyone else's.

My solution was to get somebody else to do it.

I took a step back – a big step back, and I took my hands off every situation that did not pertain to me. I let God be God, and I went back to being Rhonda. I started paying closer attention to the life that should matter to me the most – mine – and I let God handle everyone and everything else.

Retire the Know It All

There's no human who has all the answers. And despite what you may think and what you may believe others think, no one truly expects you to do it all and to have all the answers. Carrying the weight of that expectation is unreasonable and unfair. The best thing we can do for ourselves is to get comfortable with three words.

I. Don't. Know.

In addition to the word "no", people need to get used to hearing "I don't know" from us, so they can stop expecting us to drop what we're doing to solve their problems. It's also how we can release ourselves from the handcuffs of feeling that we must be everyone's all-in-one solution. We are not every woman. It is not all in us. Get somebody else to do it.

In truth, we don't even have to know who knows the answers. All we need is the understanding that the responsibility of mentally and emotionally lifting everyone's burdens isn't ours to bear.

We're in the Age of Information. Nearly anything we want to know or learn can be discovered, oftentimes for no cost at all. There's absolutely nothing wrong with allowing those resources to be used and allowing others to learn and grow in ways that benefit them immediately and in the long term.

Of course, I am not saying that you should never provide your input, when it's appropriate to do so. I am saying that we must know our capacity for the number of problems we can solve and the number of people we can rescue. It simply cannot be everyone in every circle we're in. And so, we have to re-teach people how to engage with us. Rather than answering every question that's lobbied at you – practice saying, "I don't know. Look it up." Or, "I'm not sure, and I don't have time to look into it." In other words, I don't know; find somebody else to do it.

A quick tip for retiring the know-it-all: *check your circles*. If you're the smartest person in every room you're in and if everyone looks up to you and is pulling on you for guidance, advice, and answers, you need to ditch those spaces and find bigger ones.

Instead, find groups of people who are where you want to be – people who can mentor and serve as role models for you. Every leader needs a leader, and every brilliant person needs to belong to a community of people more brilliant than they are. Certainly, it will be uncomfortable at first – similar to how it felt transitioning from high school to college. As a senior, you were the "grownup", the one the freshmen looked up to. That following year, though, as a first-year college student, you were back to being the little fish in the big pond. It was an ego-check, indeed.

Likewise, in these new rooms, your "I don't know" will not only give you the opportunity to listen and learn, they will also give you the chance to be challenged and to grow. You'll finally have places where you can be poured into and discover what it feels like to have value added to you, rather than always being the one adding all the value.

"I don't know" releases us from the belief that our value comes from how much we know and how well we can meet people's expectations of us – whether those expectations are real or not. It also helps us rid ourselves of our perfectionistic tendencies and allows us to be exactly what we are – human. To use those three words effectively, however, we must keep in mind that there's absolutely nothing we can do about other people's reactions to our decisions.

There's a saying: "Your opinion of me is not my problem". The sooner we can adopt that statement as more than a t-shirt slogan or a social media meme, the sooner we'll be able to unapologetically declare that we don't know, we don't have to know, and – honestly – we don't want to know.

Give Them Their Stuff Back

For me, adopting "no", "I don't know", and "get somebody else to do it" into my lexicon allowed me to mind more of my own business. I stopped answering questions and giving unsolicited advice, and I stopped trying to be a savior to everyone in my life. In doing so, I discovered something miraculous: people can (and will) figure their own stuff out. They didn't need me thinking or worrying for them. I realized that as fully grown adults, they could handle their own lives, and it didn't matter whether they could do it as well as me or not. I didn't have to live with their decisions.

It is not my role to keep the people around me out of the pitfalls of life. Certainly, if I am able to warn them, pray for them, and give advice that will help them avoid making unnecessary mistakes, I should do that. But I've learned that I should not, under any circumstances, continuously sacrifice my peace for their comfort. It doesn't help them or me in the long run.

In the Bible, Jesus tells his disciples that the second commandment is to "love your neighbor as yourself." Many times, we catch the "love your neighbor" part but overlook the "as yourself" at the end. Those two words remind us that we can only love others to the extent that we love ourselves. And if we look at the definition of love, we find that it is patient, kind, doesn't envy, doesn't boast, and isn't proud. It does not dishonor, it is not self-seeking, it is not easily angered, and it keeps no record of wrongs. Love is not happy when others fail but rejoices with the truth. It always protects, always trusts, always hopes, and always perseveres.

It's easy to point that definition in the direction of others, as a measurement of how they should treat us or how we should treat them. But we don't use it on ourselves enough. Nowhere in that description does it say that love requires the relinquishing of our peace or our health, and it certainly doesn't say that we must allow self-abuse by neglecting our needs or by allowing ourselves to be taken advantage of. So, if we are improperly loving ourselves, our idea of loving others will always be off kilter. We're only able to give love to the extent we have love for ourselves.

I said in an earlier chapter that for something to be sacrificed, it must first die. Every time we sacrifice ourselves for others, it's a form of suicide – we are slowly, surely killing ourselves. The stress, the angst, the immune disorders, the depression – they're all conditions that can result from being in a constant state of stress, what mental health professionals call fight, flight, or freeze. Those states have great benefits in the short term, when they're protecting us from real, imminent danger. Under prolonged conditions, though, they're deadly.

Not only do they wreak havoc on our mental health, they can cause all kinds of devastation in our professional and personal lives. Our relationships suffer, we lose our zest for life, and we feel overwhelmed and resentful all the time. And, while we may be frustrated with the fact that the world isn't revolving in sync with our demands, our deepest frustration is with ourselves. We see that we are overly involved in other peoples' lives but our toxic need to feel useful and to be helpful keep us from letting go.

There is nothing wrong with releasing yourself from the role of "savior". So, when you find yourself in a place where you're being overtaken by the cares and concerns of others – to the extent that you can't even care for yourself – it's ok to return those cares to their rightful owners.

I once heard Steve Harvey say that he stopped immediately replying to voice mails and text messages from people asking him for money. Instead, he said, he waits days or weeks to reply, and then asks, "How'd it all turn out?" What he found was that inevitably, the person had found a solution, or the situation had worked itself out without his intervention.

That's not a fairy-tale solution that only applies to the rich and famous. Help may indeed be needed, but it's not always your job to provide it. Before you take on one more care that isn't yours to carry, stop and think. Ask yourself if you really have the mental capacity to worry about one more thing. Determine whether the issue is truly yours to be up-all-night worried about. Be honest about whether you'll be helping them, but damaging you.

Be reminded that your strength isn't determined by how much "stuff" you can carry and keep walking. It doesn't reflect how much pain you can take without asking for relief, nor is it a measure of the extent to which you can give without receiving anything in return. Your strength doesn't make you a good person, nor does it make you more loveable or likeable.

The love of others cannot be earned through our display of strength. They won't love us more if we are more involved in their lives and their decision making. We cannot earn more respect by micromanaging our loved ones through their challenges. At some point, we must realize that we do them and ourselves a favor by taking our hands off the situation and letting them and God figure things out.

When we commit to loving and protecting ourselves first, saying "no" becomes easier, and we put ourselves in a better position to recognize when our peace, our mental health, and our resources have been stretched to their limits. That self-love will make us take a step back and set appropriate boundaries, so we can be supportive in ways that don't leave us in a deficit.

The great thing about saying "no" and allowing "someone else to do it" is that we don't have to find the "someone else". All we have to do is recognize that the "someone" isn't us.

CHAPTER 15

My Secret: I'm Lonely

The Truth: I Need You

There's a question that pops up on social media from time to time: "What's harder for you? Saying I love you, I'm sorry, or I need help?"

For me, the answer is admitting that I need help or that I need someone. It stumps me every time. In all honesty, I say it so infrequently that when I do utter the words "I need you", people come running like it's a 3-alarm fire.

Admitting that I need help puts me in a position of vulnerability. To say that I have a need means that I recognize the presence of a deficiency. As someone who has spent many years telling and signaling to people that I don't need anyone, those three words are scary.

The irony was that while I proudly carried the weight of "doing it all", I was secretly wishing I didn't have to. But I couldn't seem to get past the disappointment of counting on people who'd let me down and the pain of being loyal to people who didn't really deserve it. And so, I'd taken control of everything out of a need to not only get things done, but to also make sure that I didn't get hurt again in the process.

But then, it became a habit I couldn't break and ultimately a way of life. Once I discovered that I could literally accomplish anything I wanted, I believed that I didn't need help at all. I discovered that my wholeness did not depend on the presence of others. And I was right about that part. But I also noticed I'd done so much to exist without them, that I didn't have people around me who complemented me – who added to my greatness and happiness and allowed me to do the same in return.

There were few people (and sometimes no one) with whom I could share my most intimate desires, challenges, and accomplishments. It was hard to feel safe enough to share my fears and insecurities. As much as I wanted to open up to the people around me, I found it difficult to do so out of fear of becoming the next hot topic for gossip, or worse – being shunned or ignored.

Safe Is Boring

So, we tell ourselves things like, "It's hard to make friends at this big age" or "I just prefer to stay to myself", because we've raised walls around our hearts to protect them from experiencing the hurt and disappointment we experienced in the past. We have a hard time believing someone when they say they love us, because we don't trust ourselves to allow the right people in.

It's a logical conclusion to keep out as many people as possible; it's the only way for our heart to be safe. And for a while, it works – until it doesn't anymore. When we start to realize that "safe" is boring and dealing with people at a surface level and only engaging in small talk feels repetitive and pointless. We find ourselves starved for intimacy and craving stimulating conversations with people who truly get us.

It's nearly impossible to make the kinds of meaningful connections we desire without coming from behind our emotional barriers. And the "one way" connections we try to build, where we give, but never receive, don't work either. People quickly notice when they're always sharing with us, but we rarely share with them.

I can't tell you the number of times I've been called out for this: A family member or friend calls and asks how I'm doing, and instead of replying honestly – that I'm feeling low – I respond with, "I'm ok, but how are YOU?" This, of course, flips the entire conversation so the focus is placed back on the caller, and not on me or my feelings. At best, it is unfair of me to always expect others to share with me the vulnerability I refuse to share with them. At worst, it is manipulative.

In those moments, when the caller has figured out what I'm attempting to do and makes me answer, it feels odd to talk about myself and my problems. In the back of my mind, I'm wondering whether they're truly interested in what's bothering me or if they're just being polite. It's difficult for me to believe that someone could *want* to be the same safe space for me as I've been for them.

This was my way of coping with my lack of trust in people, and I'm certainly not alone. Most of the time, as strong Black women, we're not just private people who keep to ourselves, we're actively denying entry into our lives and feelings because we're skeptical about whether people will handle us and what we share with care. It's not easy for a woman who's been labeled strong to admit that she's sensitive. I can say that with confidence. It is much easier to feed into the hype that we're tough and that we can take anything life throws at us.

The hard part is letting people know when the blows we've been dealt have caused damage, when the challenges we're facing seem like they may get the best of us, or when we're going through a season where we feel demeaned, demoralized, and discouraged. Those are the hardest things for strong women to share, because we fear that when people realize we have insecurities, that we're terrified, or that we're feeling defeated, they'll judge us, ridicule us, or abandon us.

It's much easier to uphold the pretense that we're fine. Even though we wish we felt safe enough to completely fall apart and not have to worry about being admonished to pick ourselves up, push forward, or be ok, the reality is: we can't bring ourselves to do it. There's too much of a risk. We wouldn't be able to handle it if we shared our heart with one more person who left us feeling dismissed, ignored, or misunderstood. It's painful to carry it all alone, but not as painful as thinking we've discovered a safe place only to realize we were wrong.

Open the Door

One of the most life-giving discoveries you can make is the realization that there are indeed people in your world who think you're amazing and who want to love you. These people will protect your heart without question. They will see you, and they will hold space for you to be fully you. The only thing they will require of you is that you let them in – that you allow them to be for you what you are for them and for others.

These are the people who will pour back into you and who will help you make sure that your cup stays full. These people will have the capacity to reciprocate, and they won't be content to just receive from you. They will challenge you to truly connect with them and they'll show you that they see and value you.

In our new definition of strength, we're rejecting the notion that we are the only ones we can trust and rely on. We're realizing that like a braided cord, we are stronger in relationships – in partnerships. From a business perspective, one of the measures we evaluate when determining the growth potential of a firm is the strength of its team. It is well known that a business will only grow to a limited point when it is led and run by a singular person. But, when a company is led by a team of people with varying strengths, experiences, and points of view, its potential for success skyrockets. No one person is responsible for all the tasks, all the knowledge, and all the output for the entire firm. The possibilities for the firm's long-term growth and success are vastly improved.

The same principle applies to our personal lives. We must recognize that while we can stack thousands of tasks, responsibilities, and concerns on our shoulders and carry them successfully, there's only so much we can carry, for so long, and only so far. At some point we reach capacity – or a breaking point. It is much easier to carry all those things when we allow others to help us. With redefined strength, our power comes from our ability to connect and collaborate, rather than our propensity to isolate. As strong Black women, our strength is in numbers more than the individual. The statement, "We're stronger together" is more than a slogan; it's truth. You can grow faster and go farther when you leverage the power of the collective.

Being strong means shedding the idea that we're the only ones we can count on to get things done, and we'll have to release the belief that we're best off alone. What we must find is the reassurance that the people we do allow close to us are indeed those who deserve to be there. We'll have to admit that we not only want help; we need help. That we're tired of doing everything on our own and playing all the parts in this movie called life. Be honest! We desire companionship, love, and friendship, and we no longer want to provide it all for ourselves, by ourselves.

Getting to the point where you're able to make those deep connections can be a challenge, but you don't have to jump off the cliff without a parachute. To start, you must first regain trust in yourself. You've got to believe that regardless of however poor judge of character you may have been in the past, any painful dealings you may have had with toxic people were not a result of your bad judgment; they were a result of a toxic person's toxic actions.

And that's an important acknowledgment because there's nothing you can do about the behavior of a toxic person, other than to use their behavior to help you identify red flags in the future. You should be mindful that not all nice people are good people. You're not the only one who has been deceived into thinking that someone who people considered to be nice or fun to be around was a good person. That's not always the case, so you can forgive yourself if you were duped by their act.

The process of determining whether someone is a safe space for you requires discernment and the willingness to take a bit of risk. You won't have to blow up all your emotional walls today, but you will have to take down a few bricks so you can peek out and new people can peek in. The only way you can determine whether someone is genuine with their intentions is to let them show you, rather than simply assuming that everyone's intentions are bad. In doing so, you give yourself the opportunity to collect evidence that the people assigned to your future will not handle you the same as the people from your past.

Trust must be built on facts, not feelings. This means that, if we're going to be fair, the new people in our lives should not have to pay for the bad behavior of the folks who were there before them. Certainly, we have intuition, but it should contextualize the facts we're being faced with. Your intuition is there to holler, "No, girl! I know you see that those flags are red!" But it should not be the voice that keeps you from opening up ever.

Not everyone is going to let you down, but the unspoken fear for many of us is: we never know who's who upfront. But as my beloved friend and coach, Doug Stampfli, once said, "It's true you can't pour from an empty vessel, Rhonda, but it can't be refilled if you won't take the lid off."

While we should certainly be observant and cautious with our hearts, we must take care not to remain closed to the people we should allow in. Otherwise, we'll miss out on valuable connections due to our scrutiny and skepticism. Our challenge now is discerning whom to trust and allowing them to enter and take up space in our lives. Yes, there are risks, but when we take the chance, we'll unlock the level of living we've been dreaming of.

Chapter 16

My Secret: I Don't Belong Here

The Truth: I'm Exactly Where I'm Supposed to Be

The healing I found while discovering and releasing my hidden pain allowed me to see that I am not an imposter. It opened my eyes to the fact that I had been battling between two people – one who was confident and well put together and the other who wasn't permitted to see the light of day.

Although the confident one had the courage to show up in public, it was the other one who was pulling all the strings backstage. She was the one who had convinced me that people would think I wasn't who I claimed to be and that it was only a matter of time before everyone viewed me as a fraud.

As I learned more about her, though, I discovered that she was doing all she'd ever known. Her role in the background was to catalog each secret and lock it away. And while the events that happened may have ended up forgotten, she never forgot one detail about what took place and how she felt. She was the one who reminded me of my flaws and all the ways they'd allowed me to be hurt.

She was always waiting for the "other shoe" to drop, and she never felt like she was safe or secure. As my unhealed self, she pushed me to seek validation anywhere I could find it – from family, friends, and peers because she needed constant reassurance that I measured up to their standards and everyone else's. She was constantly on the lookout for competition – always pushing me to be the best – because she believed that if we performed just right, people would finally respect and accept us, and everything would be ok.

But this version of me was misinformed. She didn't know that I didn't have to be ruled by insecurity and fear. Because she was so broken and unhealed, she couldn't understand that the things she had experienced and the things she knew about me didn't make me unlovable.

She was ruled by emotion – namely fear – which caused her to react in protective mode any time someone got close to discovering who I truly am. It was her job to protect me from being hurt again. So, when situations would arise that appeared to match previous times in my life when I'd been hurt or abused, she'd speak up and warn me that I was about to be hurt like I had before. Or that I didn't belong in the space I was in.

She was doing the best she could with what she had – a long history of pain, rejection, and abuse – and she was making decisions for me from the perspective of her pain. I can't be angry with her for that.

As I unpacked each of my secrets and discovered the unhealed pain that was flowing beneath them, I was finally able to see her point of view. The times she'd whisper "You don't belong here" weren't meant to make me feel inadequate or insecure, like I'd thought. They were her way of communicating to me that I was in an unknown place, and for us, "the unknown" is bad. She was reminding me that the unknown is where people had hurt me – where I'd been passed over and rejected. She was truly afraid of what would happen if the pains of our past were repeated. She didn't want that for me, so the only thing she could do was tell me I didn't belong and urge me to get out.

My healing uncovered the truth that I could be the one calling the shots and not my unhealed self. I didn't need her protection anymore, nor did I want it. But I knew I had to do something about her voice. I didn't want to silence her the way she'd silenced me, but it was clear she could no longer be the one doing all the talking. So, rather than shutting her up, I had a talk with her.

I closed my eyes and visualized her – she was beautiful, and she was battered. On her body were the scars of every emotional hit I'd ever taken. All the times I'd been cut, she was the one who'd bled. She was weary, but there was a fire in her eyes that let me know it didn't matter how much she had to carry – she was prepared to do whatever it took to protect me.

I took a long look at her, I gathered her tattered hands in mine, and told her, "I'm sorry." I apologized to her for all the times I heaped more on her than I should have – for all the times I added to her pain and made her feel that she didn't matter. I told her I was sorry for the ways I'd mistreated her by not giving her time and space to heal when I knew she'd been hurt, and I told her I was going to do my part to change all that.

I thanked her for simply wanting to protect me from rejection, and I acknowledged that I knew she wasn't purposely trying to make me feel like an imposter. Then, I told her that protecting me wasn't her job anymore – that it was time for us to heal and from here on out, I'd be taking care of her.

You Have Permission to Heal

For so long, I had allowed fear to make me believe that I was a fraud, but as I was healing, I replayed some of the painful events and realized that none of them made me an imposter. Not one of them proved that I wasn't fully equipped and capable of overcoming whatever I faced. Even when

I'd faced my most difficult days, what I wasn't able to do, God stepped in and made up the difference.

I really had to run my resumé for my misinformed self. I had to remind her that I'd survived everything I'd faced – that I'd endured the toughest of times and not one of them had gotten the best of me. That when the lions, tigers, and bears showed up to devour me, I fought them all and won.

This is how I claimed the courage to look at myself in the mirror and declare that I am exactly where I'm supposed to be. Everything I have been through has ultimately worked for my good. Even the bad judgement calls and the mistakes I have made equipped me to thrive at this exact moment in time. There wouldn't be a book to write about healing secret pain if I'd never been hurt. I wouldn't be able to share experiences I haven't had.

There came a point in my healing journey when I realized that much of what I'd been through wasn't for me. It wasn't to harm me or even to benefit me. It was to inform me. It was to plant in me the compassion and understanding I'd need to write this book, so I could not only share my secrets but so that you'd know you're not alone. And that if I could go through terrible times and come out on the other side better than I was when I went in, you can too.

You're not an imposter. You belong in every room God places your feet in. The things you have survived weren't meant to give you an imposter complex. That was a trick of the enemy. They were meant to prepare you for your purpose.

As long as your unhealed self has the reins, she's always going to rule you based on her fear. She's going to insist that you're unprepared, unworthy, and undeserving. And the way you'll stop her whispering won't be to find ways to drown her out and out-work her. You'll have to heal her – to reassure her feelings and fears with facts and logic and to remind her that you're not that little girl or that younger version of yourself anymore, who didn't know what to do to protect or help herself.

You can tell her that she doesn't have to hold on to those secrets, nor does she have to be strong for you. She can set it all down and everything will be ok. You can give her permission to rest and finally heal.

***

That's how releasing imposter syndrome starts – by refusing to allow your pain to control you any longer. What makes those words transformative and not just affirmations you say to yourself is your willingness to deal with the secrets. You won't be able to simply affirm your way out of this; you have to actively do the restorative work.

You'll have to take the tarp off those old emotional crates and dig all the way to the bottom of them – the root cause. Much like I did, you'll have to go back to the secret that started it all and determine whether you truly healed from it or if you healed just enough to hide it and move on.

You'll have to be willing to look honestly at the stuff you filed away in the box labeled "it doesn't matter" and see if the things in there mattered more than you thought they did. Because those are the pains that add up quietly and sneak up on you out of nowhere.

That's what happened after the election. We each discovered that over the years, we had boxed up our traumas, big and small, and simply pushed forward day after day, without revealing how deeply we'd been hurt. We forced ourselves to be ok, because that's what it took to move forward. We used our strength to pretend we were unfazed and appear as though we weren't holding back an impulse to wring someone's neck.

But things have changed now. A bright light has been shone on the pain we were secretly carrying, and we realize that we don't want to keep doing what we've always done, trying to get a different result. We now understand why our misinformed selves were always yelling so loud. They could perceive that the people who could trigger our unhealed pain were in the room all along!

***

So now, here we are. We've collectively decided that we no longer want to be the ones everyone depends on for the answers and for saving their backsides. We don't want to come to anyone else's rescue. We're saving ourselves now. We're looking out for our own interests. We're discovering that despite all our help and all we've done to prove our value, when it's our time to be rescued, everyone seems to be fresh out of lifelines.

We're focusing on our healing now because it's the only way to silence the imposter syndrome and reclaim the voices we've buried for too long. Healing allows us to see that we are worthy, valuable, and lovable without needing anyone else's approval. It replaces that misinformed voice with one that reassures us that we belong, that we deserve good things, and that we're fully capable of seizing the opportunities we know are meant for us.

When we reclaim our voice, we'll fully step into our power. We won't question our place at the table anymore because we'll have no problem acknowledging that we earned our spot. We own it.

There are few greater feelings than walking into spaces you'd normally be intimidated by and thinking, *I belong here*. And it feels even better when you are unafraid to take up space – to be seen for all that you are and to be unafraid of what people may find when they see you walk by in all your brilliance.

It's A Brand-New Day

The days of shying away and backing down are over. It's time to find the courage to travel our path to real healing – to take the journey of becoming unashamed of who we are and what we've been through.

For me, the process has been completely different from what I thought it would be, but the outcome wasn't. I've found freedom. I feel lighter, empowered, emboldened. No longer do I feel the need to prove anything to anyone, and I am getting better at saying no and sticking to it. I no longer feel guilt and shame about my experiences.

Healing also opened me up to allowing new people and new opportunities in my life; I no longer feel alone in crowds, and I have developed genuine friendships with women who not only love me freely, but who make me feel safe to freely love them, too. I no longer fear loving or expressing a desire to feel loved. Best of all, my heart has been freed from the shackles of grudge-holding, and I feel more liberated than I ever have.

I arrived here because I was doing what seemed to be all the wrong things, but it's quite likely that if I'd never hit my breaking point, I may never have gone on this journey. I might have never decided to deal with all the junk I'd been carrying around, and perhaps I wouldn't be here to share my story of healing and rebirth with you.

If you asked me whether I am glad I went through what I did, I'd probably hit you with "not just nah…" But in truth, I am grateful. My experiences got me where I am; I couldn't have gotten here traveling any other path. And I would not have the testimony that I have today.

I am not a victim; I am a conqueror.

I am no longer broken; I am healed.

I am not an imposter; I am right where I belong.

And if you ask me, that's real strength.

Conclusion

At the beginning of this book, I wrote that I hoped it would give you the courage to take a look at your own life and your own secret pain. My goal wasn't just to spill tea or expose myself to the world; it was to prove that healing is possible. I wanted you to know that despite what you've been through, you don't have to carry the weight of those experiences around for the rest of your life. You can give yourself permission to rest. You can allow yourself to take care of you first. And you can take all the time you need to reclaim your power and your voice.

Most of all, I wanted you to know that while you may have had little or no control over the ways people have hurt you, you do have the ability and responsibility to heal from it. That's no one else's job. It can't be delegated to a significant other, family member, or friend. It's up to you to do the work of reclaiming your wholeness.

Now, don't get me wrong, I'm not saying you have to take this journey alone. There's no way I could have traveled this path without help. It will take a team – a village – to support you and to walk with you as you progress. I mentioned partnering with people who can hold space for you to share the events of your life without interruption or judgement. These might be friends, but they are more likely to be therapists. If you don't have one, I highly recommend getting one for this journey. You'll be surprised at what you uncover when you start going through those old memories, and you'll need someone to help you safely navigate processing those experiences.

There's no way I could have gotten through this process without my family and friends – and you will need your network too. Let them know you're on this quest for healing and allow them to serve as sounding boards for your discoveries. You'll find that when it's time for you to share your story, you'll feel much more comfortable with doing so if you've built up your confidence with people you know care about you.

Finally, this isn't a process you can go through without God's help. As the One who crafted us, and as the One who sees the big picture of all He's created throughout all time, He's the One who is best suited to give us insights regarding the things we discover when we start investigating those secrets. While I was reflecting, I'd often ask, "What was the point of that?" And in my prayers and journaling time, He'd answer.

He didn't tell me everything, though. Let me be honest about that. But I did get insights into many of the questions I had about what I'd been through, and I believe that happened because I had the courage to ask. I'm not of the belief that we shouldn't question God. There are plenty of times in the Bible when His children asked Him why, and I believe we still have that privilege today. I believe His answers to our questions help deepen our ability to believe Him and believe in Him. They also unlock our ability to move further along in our journeys as we tap into our vulnerability and authenticity.

Happily Ever After

The challenges we've faced definitely required strength to overcome them, so there's no doubt in my mind that we're strong! Today, we are wiser, more agile, more resilient, and better prepared for our future. The thing is, we don't celebrate that enough. It seems so easy for us to look back and point out all the times we failed or made poor decisions, but we rarely focus on what matters most: we overcame. There wasn't one mistake or misstep that got the best of us. Despite all we've been through, we won – and we're still winning.

The longer you cling to your secrets, the more they'll distort your view of yourself and your victories. They'll have you believing that your failures define you more than your triumphs do. And that is patently untrue. Everything you've been through has contributed to the strength you now have. You didn't endure those battles to keep them buried in shame – you endured them so you could claim your victory – over what you've already defeated and over all the other challenges to come. That's what you should cling to and then inspire others to do the same.

It's time for you to shine the light on the secrets you've been holding onto – yes, even the most painful experiences – and when you do, you'll put an end to the dual life you've been living. You won't have to pretend to be whole, knowing you're not. Instead, you'll live fully and boldly, and you'll embrace a strength that makes you feel better day by day. Best of all, you'll be free to walk in your authority and authenticity, and you'll walk right into becoming the woman you're created to be.

Acknowledgements

First, giving honor to God, who is the head of my life. Deacons, saints, and friends…

Ok, ok, ok –

Too churchy.

I'll be serious.

I couldn't have done this without a village of people cheering me on. I want to thank Dr. Synetheia Newby, not only for writing the foreword, but for pushing me to write this book in the first place. The homework assignment she gave me back in 2020 – to write my seven secrets on sticky notes – remains on the whiteboard in my office to this day. Thank you, my dear friend, for not letting me skip out on this assignment.

I also want to thank the folks who allowed me to use their ears as sounding boards, and who lovingly listened to my whining and my complaints during the writing process. They were there to encourage me when I wasn't sure I could keep going, and they celebrated every win and breakthrough I had along the way. So, a *huge* "THANK YOU" goes to Danielle Fisher, Doug Stampfli, Dr. C. Renee Greer, and Shanel Evans.

And finally, there's no way I could have written this book without my family. Daddy and Mommie – thank you so much for all your support. There are no better cheerleaders on Earth than you two. Thank you, Daddy, for your wisdom and for our conversations that pushed me to go deeper and to think bigger. I am so thankful to have you in my corner! Mommie, I appreciate you so much for all your encouragement. When you said, "Now's the time to write your book," I was hesitant – nah, I was scared! But you knew, and you were right. The time is now, and I'm *so* glad I listened! Thank you.

To my "sibs", Micahl (Tiffany) and Ben (Valerie), thank you for having my back. I love you four more than life itself. And to my daughter, Maiyah, you've always been my rock. God gave me the best gift *ever* when He gave me you.

I am so grateful to be surrounded by people who love me. And I am even more grateful that I'm able to receive that love and give it right back.

And finally, thank you, Dear Reader, for taking this journey with me. It just wouldn't have been the same without you.

About Dr. Rhonda

Dr. Rhonda Alexander is an award-winning author, entrepreneur, strategist, speaker, and coach who is dedicated to helping individuals and organizations unlock their potential. She is the founder of IUVO Consulting, LLC, a global FDA regulatory-compliance consulting firm; E^2 Entrepreneur & Executive Coaching, LLC, which focuses on the growth and development of entrepreneurs and leaders; and SoulScribe, a publishing house and coaching firm that helps industry leaders turn their expertise and stories into impactful, revenue-generating books.

Dr. Alexander holds a B.S. in Molecular Biology from Hampton University, an M.S. in Clinical Chemistry from the Medical College of Virginia/Virginia Commonwealth University, a Master of Public Administration from Old Dominion University, and a Doctorate in Strategic Leadership from Regent University. With nearly 30 years of experience leading teams, launching businesses, and consulting globally,

"Dr. Rhonda" brings a rare combination of strategic expertise and heartfelt empathy to her work in every capacity.

Beyond her professional achievements, Dr. Rhonda is a travel junkie and "mom" to Maiyah, a talented young woman who inspires her every day.

Dr. Rhonda's work has sparked transformation in individuals and organizations worldwide, helping them break through barriers, scale their impact, and turn untapped potential into measurable success. With a reputation for delivering actionable strategies and life-changing insights, Dr. Rhonda empowers her clients to redefine their futures, achieve their goals, and embrace the life they're created to live.

To learn more about Dr. Rhonda, visit her website www.thedrrhonda.com.

INVITE DR. RHONDA @ thedrrhonda.com/speaking

[f] Facebook.com/drrhondaalexander

[Instagram] Instagram: @drrhondaalexander

[in] LinkedIn.com/in/thedrrhonda

[▶] YouTube: @UnperturbedThePodcast

Become Part of Dr. Rhonda's Community: The Haven

You've started the journey—now, don't walk it alone. *The Haven* is where high-achieving Black women break free from toxic strength and step into a new kind of power, together.

Breaking free is only the beginning.

Go to www.enterthehaven.net to join.

www.ingramcontent.com/pod-product-compliance
Lightning Source LLC
Chambersburg PA
CBHW050525100526
44581CB00007B/131/J